BUILD YOUR OWN
WEBSITE
for BEGINNERS

Laura Cowan

Illustrated by Anna Wray

Designed by Vickie Robinson,
Jenny Offley and Samuel Gorham

Coding consultant: Nikolaos Papadopoulos

CONTENTS

JAVASCRIPT

USEFUL STUFF

USBORNE QUICKLINKS

To find extra resources and downloads to help you build your own website, go to **usborne.com/Quicklinks** and type in the keywords 'build your own website'.

Please follow the internet safety guidelines at the Usborne Quicklinks website. Children should be supervised online.

WHAT IS BUILDING A WEBSITE ?

Building a website means creating a set of **web pages** – documents designed to be seen and shared over the **Internet** – and linking them together. This is a great way to connect to other people, wherever they are in the world, and share information, pictures, games or whatever you want.

BUT, WHAT IS THE INTERNET?

The Internet is a gigantic network of computers around the world, working together and sharing information. Each computer in the network needs an address, a bit like a telephone number, so other computers can find it. And information has to be shared in a standard format, known as **HTTP**.

The Internet isn't just used for websites. It also streams music and movies, carries phone calls and messages, and allows people to play games with each other all over the world.

THE WORLD WIDE WEB

Together, all the websites and web pages in the world form an enormous library known as the **World Wide Web**. The Web gets its name because of the way all its parts link together, like an enormous spider's web.

Any computer anywhere can access the Web, as long as it has an internet connection and a **browser** – the program which manages the connection and displays the information going through it.

WEB WORDS

Website
A set of related web pages.

Web page
A document you can access on the **World Wide Web**.

The Internet
A network of billions of computers linked across the world.

World Wide Web
An enormous library of shared web pages.

Browser
A program which manages an internet connection and displays the information that goes through it.

HOW DO YOU BUILD A WEBSITE?

The quickest way to make a website is to use a ready-made template (see pages 90-91). But if you actually want to build YOUR OWN from scratch, you'll need to learn to code.

Coding means giving a computer clear, simple instructions in a language it understands. For a website, you need three computer languages...

WARNING

Computers follow instructions blindly – they can't think for themselves. So, in coding, everything must be spelled out clearly, leaving nothing out.

CSS

CSS stands for 'Cascading Style Sheets'. You use it to **style** or set the appearance of your web page – the colours, borders, lettering and more. You could make a website without CSS, but it wouldn't look very exciting.

JAVASCRIPT

JavaScript allows you to add mini programs called **scripts** to your pages. These scripts can animate parts of your page and make them react when you click on them.

HTML

HTML stands for 'Hypertext Markup Language'. You use it to 'mark up' or label your information, so any computer anywhere will know how to display it.

Imagine your website is a house and every web page is a different room. **HTML** builds the structure, like bricks. **CSS** is the wallpaper, carpets and decorations that make it all look nice.

If you want your house to have the latest technology, you will also need **JavaScript**.

WHAT YOU'LL FIND IN THIS BOOK

This book will help you build your own website using **HTML**, **CSS** and **JavaScript**. You will find out how to style text, add pictures, create special effects and more. Everything is broken down into short, easy-to-follow steps, and there's a glossary at the back with definitions of useful words.

GETTING STARTED

To write your own web pages, you will need a
code-writing program installed on your computer.

There are several code-writing programs
you can choose. This book uses one called
Notepad++ because it's free and easy to
use. If it's not on your computer already,
go to Usborne Quicklinks for a link and
instructions. If you want to use another
code-writing program instead, you can – it
won't change the code, but the window you
write it into will look a bit different.

Notepad++ only works on
Windows® computers. If you have a **Mac®**
computer, you need to install a different
program, such as **Smultron**. Go to Usborne
Quicklinks to find out how. You can also use
a **text editor** such as **Notepad** on Windows®
computers or **SimpleText** on Mac®.

1. If you have a Windows® computer,
open the **Start Menu**, click on **All
Programs**, and double-click on **Notepad++**.
You should see a window like this...

If you have this
icon on your screen,
you can open **Notepad++**
by double-clicking on it.

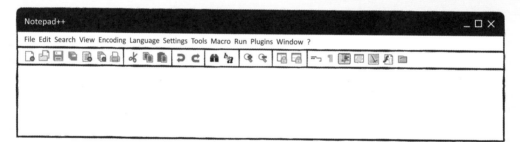

2. Click on **File** in the menu bar and
choose **Save As** in the drop-down menu.

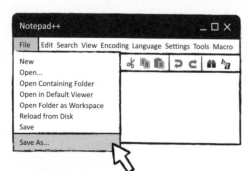

Here I go!

Save a blank file as
'gettingstarted.html'.

3. Set up a new page by typing in the code below. Be careful to type everything exactly right. Notice the column of dots – this means you need to set in the code by pressing the space bar twice.

Notepad++ will automatically put different types of instructions in different colours. It also has columns of dots, to help you line up your code.

This tells the browser what follows is in HTML.

Words in <> are known as **tags** (see below). This is your opening **<html>** tag and tells the browser you'll be working in English.

This tells the browser how to store the characters (meaning the letters, numbers and symbols you type).

```
<!DOCTYPE html>
<html lang="en">

<head>
  <meta charset="UTF-8">
  <title>My very first website</title>
</head>
```

The **<head>** tags enclose information about your page. We've separated them from the **<html>** tag by pressing the return key.

The **<title>** tags set the title of the page, which will appear at the top of the browser window.

TAGS

HTML instructions are known as **tags**. They usually come in pairs and look something like this...

<head>

The **opening tag** tells the browser where to BEGIN an instruction.

</head>

The **closing tag** tells the browser where an instruction ENDS.

It's VERY important to close tags, otherwise they won't work. You can open and close tags as you go along, or type both at once and insert the rest of your code afterwards.

4. Now, to save your page. Click on the 'Save' icon at the top of your window, or use the **keyboard shortcut** below.

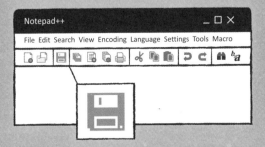

To use the **keyboard shortcut**, on a Windows® computer, hold down **Ctrl** and tap **S**, then release both. (On a Mac®, it's **Command** and **S**.)

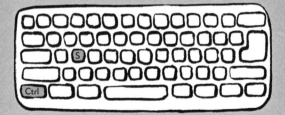

It's a good idea to save code regularly, so you don't lose any work.

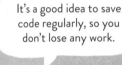

7

ADDING CONTENT

Now you've set up a page, it's time to add some content. Content is what you want people to see on your page. It could be anything – words, pictures, links to other websites...

1. Content goes between **<body></body>** tags. Underneath the closing **</head>** tag, press **return** and then add an opening **<body>** tag.

```
</head>

<body>
```

TAG NAMES

Tags are named after their jobs, so they're easier to remember – for example, **<p>** is a paragraph tag.

2. To make a heading and a paragraph of text, type this underneath the opening **<body>** tag.

> This makes a big heading.

> This makes a paragraph.

```
<body>
  <h1>Getting started with HTML</h1>
  <p>First, you need to learn about tags.</p>
```

3. You can also use tags to create a list. Type the following, using the space bar to line up your code as shown. This is known as **nesting** (see right).

> **<ul>** makes a list with bullet points. For a list with numbers, use **<ol>** . The 'ul' stands for 'unordered' list and the 'ol' for 'ordered' list.

> Each item in your list goes between **<li>** tags. 'li' stands for 'list item'.

NESTING

Nesting is when you open and close a tag inside another one. Nested tags are always **indented**. In this book, we're **indenting** by pressing the space bar twice. Each line of dots represents one indent. If you don't indent your code, it will still work, but it won't be easy for you or others to read.

```
<ul>
  <li>Header tags</li>
  <li>Paragraph tags</li>
  <li>List tags</li>
</ul>
</body>

</html>
```

> Don't forget to close your **<body>** and **<html>** tags!

Once you've typed it all in, close your tags. Then save your file again (see step 4 of 'Getting Started'). Congratulations – you've just made your first webpage!

To see it, go to the menu bar at the top, click on **Run** and select the browser you use. You should see something like this...

EVERYONE! I've made a web page!

My very first website ✕

Getting started with HTML

First, you need to learn about tags.
- Header tags
- Paragraph tags
- List tags

You can also run HTML files in your browser by double-clicking the file icon (or little picture) in its folder. The icon will look the same as the one for the browser you use.

PROBLEMS?

If you don't see ANYTHING, you probably didn't save your code. Go back to step 4 and save it again.

If the page doesn't look how you expected, look at your code carefully and compare it line by line with the code in the steps. Check you've closed all your tags and copied all the code exactly. Lots of coding mistakes are caused by typing errors.

All the code in this book is available on Quicklinks for you to download and check your own against.

TIDY CODE

If your lines of code start getting too long, click on **View** in the menu bar and select **Word wrap**. This will keep your code to the size of the window, so you can see it all at once.

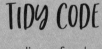

View

Always on Top
Toggle Full Screen Mode
Post-It
Show Symbol
Zoom
Move/Clone Current Document
Tab

Word wrap

EXTRA HEADERS

So far, you've only used one heading or **header** size, but HTML has six – plus a few other ways to change how text looks.

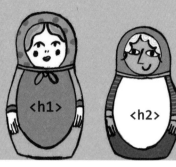

1. To try out some different headings, go back to your HTML document and change the **<p>** tags to **<h2>** with the following text.

```
<body>
  <h1>Getting started with HTML</h1>
  <h2>Headers are an easy way to change the size of text.</h2>
```

2. Now, delete everything between **</h2>** and the closing **</body>** tag, and type the text highlighted in yellow...

```
<body>
  <h1>Getting started with HTML</h1>
  <h2>Header tags are an easy way to change the size of text.</h2>
  <h3>There are six sizes.</h3>
  <h4>The higher the number the smaller the heading.</h4>
  <h5>The smallest headers are <em> REALLY </em><small> small</small>.</h5>
  <h6>But, this is the smallest they get.</h6>
</body>

</html>
```

> This emphasizes text.

> This makes text, um, small.

<h1> is the biggest header size.

<h6> is the smallest.

10

3. Make sure you've closed all your tags and saved the file. Then go back to the menu bar at the top, click on **Run** and select your usual web browser. You should see...

*My website **WILL** be the best.*

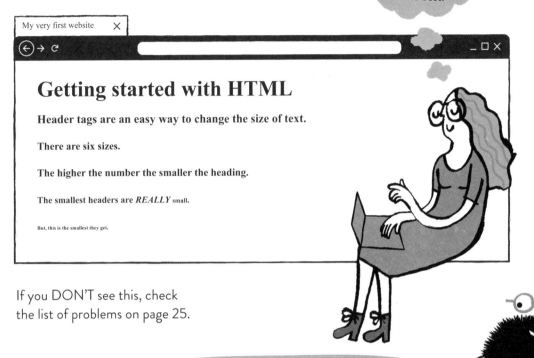

Getting started with HTML

Header tags are an easy way to change the size of text.

There are six sizes.

The higher the number the smaller the heading.

The smallest headers are *REALLY* small.

But, this is the smallest they get.

If you DON'T see this, check the list of problems on page 25.

MAKE A TEMPLATE

All HTML documents need the same opening code. Making a **template** containing this code means you won't have to type it out every time.

1. Open a file in Notepad++ and type in this code. ⟶

2. Save the file as 'template.html'. Then, when you want to start a new page, open it and save it again, giving it a new name each time.

```
<!DOCTYPE html>
<html lang="en">

<head>
  <meta charset="UTF-8">
  <title></title>
</head>

<body>
</body>

</html>
```

PLANNING YOUR WEBSITE

Now you've made a few basic pages and a template, it's time to get started on a whole website. It helps to plan out what you want before you start coding.

There are all sorts of websites – from online shops to fansites to information pages. Our website is going to be for a community space, but you can change the details to make yours about whatever you want.

1. The first thing is to decide what you want your website to include. All sites need a **homepage** – the first page everyone sees.

For our site, we're also going to create a 'What's on' page with a timetable of activities, a 'Videos' page, a 'Links' page with links to other websites, and a 'Pictures' page with a slideshow of images.

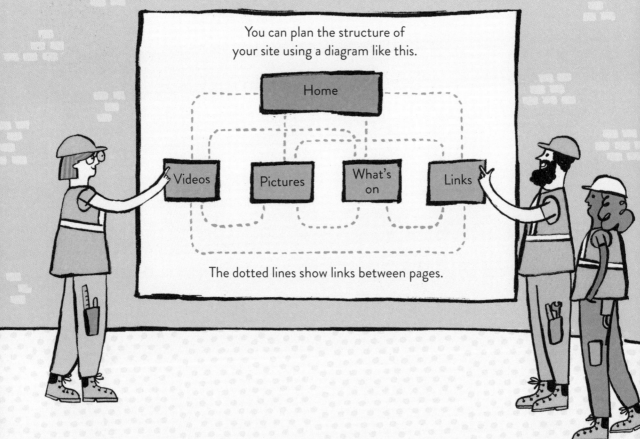

You can plan the structure of your site using a diagram like this.

Home

Videos Pictures What's on Links

The dotted lines show links between pages.

2. Next it's a good idea to sketch out a rough idea of how you want the pages to look.

Usually all the pages within a website follow a similar design, so you only need one sketch.

This is what we sketched for our website.

See pages 48 and 51 for more tips on website design.

The **banner** is a large image that goes across the top of the page. It usually contains the name of the site.

FOX HILL COMMUNITY SPACE

VIDEOS   PICTURES   WHAT'S ON   LINKS

WELCOME

Buttons are small boxes or pictures you can click on to take you to another page of the site.

The main image will go here.

This will be the text introducing the site.

A **wallpaper** is a decorative background.

3. Now it's time to start building your site. Turn the page to begin...

13

STARTING YOUR WEBSITE

Your website will have several pages and lots
of images, meaning more files to organize. It's a good
idea to begin by making a folder to store them all.

1. Right-click on the desktop (the screen you see when
your computer starts up). Click on **New** and a menu
will pop up. Then click on **Folder**.

| View |
| Sort by |
| Group by |
| Refresh |
| Customize this folder... |
| Paste |
| Paste shortcut |
| Undo Copy |
| Share with |
| New |

| Folder |
| Shortcut |
| Contact |
| Microsoft Office Word Document |
| Microsoft Office PowerPoint Presentation |
| Text Document |
| Microsoft Office Excel Worksheet |
| Compressed (zipped) Folder |
| Briefcase |

Let's call her
#@$%^J77$!

2. You should now see a 'New
Folder' icon. Right-click on
it and select **Rename File**.
Then type in a name. Choose
something that will help you
remember what's in it – for
example 'My Website'. You
can save all the files for your
website in here.

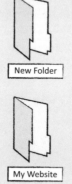

New Folder

My Website

NAMING TIPS

Keep names short
and easy to type.

Keep names sensible. If a file
name describes the file, it will
help you remember – and other
people work out – what it is.

Avoid spaces and special
characters, such as **?** and **!** .
They will confuse browsers
and search engines.

3. You also need a folder for your image files.
Open your 'My Website' folder. Right-click
inside it and create another folder in the same
way. Call this one 'Images'. Now, you can save
all the image files for your website here.

CREATING YOUR HOMEPAGE

1. Now to start making your **homepage**. Open your template and save a copy in the 'My Website' folder, renaming it 'index.html'.

2. To add pictures, you'll need image files. To use the same images as us, go to Usborne Quicklinks, follow the instructions to download them, and save or move the files to your 'Images' folder. You can also use your own – just make sure to change the links in the code to match the file names.

3. Go back to Notepad++ and insert the title of your page between the **\<title\>\</title\>** tags.

```
<!DOCTYPE html>
<html lang="en">

<head>
  <meta charset="UTF-8">
  <title>Fox Hill Community Space</title>
</head>
```

4. After the opening **\<body\>** tag, type the code below to add a banner to the top of the page.

DID YOU KNOW..?

The main HTML file for every website is usually the homepage and is ALWAYS named 'index.html'.

This page is displayed automatically when someone types in the website's address.

You can call your page whatever you like (but probably not #@$%^J77$).

The **\<section\>** tag is a way of dividing up your page.

This bit tells the browser WHERE to find the image file. The folder name is 'images'. 'banner' is the name of the file. 'png' is a type of image file. If you're using your own image, change the code here.

If you don't put a folder name, the browser will automatically look in the same folder as the HTML file.

```
<body>
  <section>
    <img src="images/banner.png">
```

The **\<img\>** tag only has one part, so you don't need to close it later.

'src' is an **attribute** – something that tells you more about an HTML **element** or **tag**. This one tells the browser that what follows is an address.

5. Add a second picture below the site banner by typing in this.

```
<img src="images/header.png">
```

Notepad++ puts different types of code in different colours. Tags are blue. Attributes are red. Anything between inverted commas (" ") is purple.

6. Now it's time to introduce your website. Type the following and close your **<section>** tags.

```
<p>Welcome to the Fox Hill Community Space website. From art to music to ping
pong, you will find out everything you need to know about our community space
and what goes on here.</p>
<p>Make yourself at HOME on our homepage and have fun exploring the site.</p>
</section>
```

7. Finally, add a **footer** at the bottom or FOOT of your page, like this. Then close your **<body>** and **<html>** tags.

```
<footer>Made by A. Fox</footer>
</body>

</html>
```

A **footer** usually contains information about who made the page, contact information, or a site map.

8. Save your work and run your file in your browser. This is what you should see...

Welcome to the Fox Hill Community Space website. From art to music to ping pong, you will find out everything you need to know about our community space and what goes on here. Make yourself at HOME on our homepage and have fun exploring the site. Made by A. Fox

LINKING PAGES

Now, you're going to make a new page with links
to other sites – and link it to your homepage.

1. Open your template
and save a new copy named
'links.html' in your website folder.

2. Give your new page a title by typing between the two **<title>** tags.

```
<title>Fox Hill Links</title>
```

3. You're going to add the banner to the top of your page again, but this time
it's also going to be a link to your homepage. Type this after the first **<body>** tag.

```
<body>
  <section>
   <a href="index.html"><img src="images/banner.png"></a>
```

The 'a' stands
for 'anchor'.

This **<img>** tag will become a link you can click on.

'href' is an **attribute** that tells the browser where the link is.

This adds
a link.

4. Type in the following to add a second link.

This adds ordinary text.

```
<p>Here are links to websites recommended by Fox Hill Community Space.</p>
<a href="https://www.usborne.com">Click here to find out where Fox Hill
Community Space gets the books for their library...</a>
```

The text in black
is what you'll see
on the page.

TYPES OF LINKS

Web addresses are known as 'urls'. A link to another page
on the same website is known as a **relative url**. Think of your
website as a family – each page is a 'relative' of the other pages.

A link to a separate site is an **absolute url**. For these
you need to add **http://** or **https://** before the address.

5. You can add as many links as you like. Just make sure to add a line break in between each one. If you don't, the links will appear on one line.

This adds a line break ('br' is short for 'break').

```
<a href="https://www.usborne.com">Click here to find out where Fox
Hill Community Space gets the books for their library...</a>
<br>
<a href="https://www.youtube.com/user/UsbornePublishing">Click here to
watch some GROOVY videos...</a>
<br>
<a href="https://www.usborne.com/quicklinks/">
This is a link to a site full of links...</a>
```

6. Close your **<section>** tag and add a footer. Then, make sure you've closed your **<body>** and **<html>** tags, save your work and close the file.

You can add as many links as you want.

```
</section>
<footer>Made by A. Fox</footer>
</body>

</html>
```

7. Open your original homepage again. For now, you're going to add a fox image you can click on to go to your links page. Type this line of code before the footer.

```
<p>Make yourself at HOME on our homepage and have fun exploring the site.<p>
<a href="links.html"><img src="images/fox.png"></a>
</section>
<footer>Made by A. Fox</footer>
</body>

</html>
```

This is a 'relative' link because it links to another page on the same site.

8. Save your 'index.html' file and run it in your browser.

It should look the same as before, but when you click on the picture of the fox you should see your new links page, as below...

Welcome to the Fox Hill Community Space website. From art to music to ping pong, you will find out everything you need to know about our community space and what goes on here.

Make yourself at HOME on our homepage and have fun exploring the site.

Made by A. Fox

Click on the fox to see the links page.

Click here on the Fox Hill banner to go back to the homepage.

Here are links to websites recommended by Fox Hill Community Space.
Click here to find out where Fox Hill Community Space gets the books for their library...
Click here to watch some GROOVY videos...
This is a link to a site full of links...

Click on any of these to go to other sites.

LOOKING GOOD

Find out how to make your pages look fancy by adding **CSS**. This is known as 'styling'.

1. First, you need to tell the browser you want to use CSS by adding a pair of **\<style>** tags before your closing **\<head>** tag. Open your 'index.html' file and add the following.

```
<style></style>
</head>
```

2. You're going to style your whole page – meaning everything between the **\<body>\</body>** tags. You can have a repeating image in the background, known as **wallpaper**, OR a coloured background. If you want to add wallpaper, type the code below.

> This tells the computer to style everything between the **\<body>** tags in your HTML file.

```
<title>Fox Hill Community Space</title>
<style>
  body {
    background-image: url("images/bg.png");
    background-repeat: repeat;
  }
</style>
```

> This adds a background image. The bit in brackets tells the browser where to find it.

> This makes the background image repeat again and again.

CSS BASICS

Rules – a rule is a complete section of CSS. For example...

Selector   Declaration

```
h1 {
    color:blue;
}
```

Property   Value

Elements – in CSS, HTML tags are referred to as elements.

Selectors – these select the element you want to style.

Declarations – each one goes on a separate line with curly brackets { } above and below, and has a semicolon ; at the end.

Properties – these are things you can style, such as colour or size.

If you'd like a colour, type the code below. There are plenty of colours to choose from. You could try HoneyDew, Fuschia or SteelBlue, or go to page 37 for even more choices.

```
<style>
  body {
    background-color: Aqua;
  }
<style>
```

HTML and CSS use American English, so 'colour' is spelled 'color'.

Colour names are **case-sensitive**, so you need to type them with upper and lower case letters exactly as you see them here.

3. To set how the text is going to look, including the size and the font or style of the letters, add two more properties and their values before your closing **}**.

```
    font-family: Calibri;
    font-size: 20px;
  }
</style>
```

This sets the font's size in pixels (see right). 20px is a good easy-to-read size for text.

PIXELS

px stands for **pixels** – the dots which make up everything on a screen. The more pixels there are, the more detailed and accurate the image.

FUN WITH FONTS

A **font** is a style of lettering – meaning the way the letters are written. Choosing a font is a simple way to personalise your site.

The fonts on the right are known as **web-safe** fonts. Web-safe means a font all computers have.

4. Wallpapers and colours look good, but it's hard to read words on top of them. So, you'll need to add a box behind your text. To tell the browser where the box goes, add an opening **<div>** tag after your opening **<body>** tag. Add a closing **<div>** tag before the closing **<body>** tag, too, and set in everything inside the **<div>** tags with two spaces.

> **<div>** tags are a way of dividing a page into sections for styling with CSS – 'div' is short for 'division'.

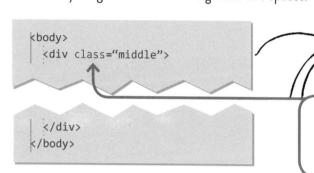

```
<body>
  <div class="middle">
```

```
  </div>
</body>
```

> A **class** is a name for a tag. Giving a tag a name means you can style JUST that tag. We've named this one 'middle', because it's in the middle of the page, but you can call it whatever you want.

5. Now to add the box itself. Go back to your **<style</style>** tags and add this after the last curly bracket.

> This is the **class** of the **<div>** tag and the **element** you want to style. It has a full stop in front of it here to show it's not a tag on its own.

```
}

.middle {
  width: 45%;
  margin: auto;
  background: white;
}
```

> This makes the box nearly half as wide as the rest of the page.

> Each CSS declaration is separated by **;** .

> This centres the box.

> We made our box white, but you can make it any colour you want – as long as you can read the words on top.

6. Finally, style the pictures and text between your **<section></section>** tags. Then save your file.

> Everything between these tags will be full width.

```
section {
  width: 100%;
  padding-bottom: 10px;
}
section img {
  width: 100%;
}
```

> This adds 10px of space between the bottom of the **<section>** tags and the footer below it.

> The 'img' styles any images between the **<section>** tags. They will be displayed at their full width.

7. Your finished code should look like this.
Check you've typed everything correctly.

```html
<!DOCTYPE html>
<html lang="en">

<head>
  <meta charset="UTF=8">
  <title>Fox Hill Community Space</title>
  <style>
    body {
      background-image: url("images/bg.png");
      background-repeat: repeat;
      font-family: Calibri;
      font-size: 20px;
    }
    .middle {
      width: 45%;
      margin: auto;
      background: white;
    }
    section {
      width: 100%;
      padding-bottom: 10px;
    }
    section img {
      width: 100%;
    }
  </style>
</head>

<body>
  <div class="middle">
    <section>
      <img src="images/banner.png">
      <img src="images/header.png">
      <p>Welcome to the Fox Hill Community Space website. From art to
      music to ping pong, you will find out everything you need to know about
      our community space and what goes on here.</p>
      <p>Make yourself at HOME on our homepage and have fun exploring the
      site.<p>
      <a href="links.html"><img src="images/fox.png"></a>
    </section>
    <footer>Made by A. Fox</footer>
  </div>
</body>

</html>
```

8. Finally, save your page and run it in your browser.
This is what you should see if you used the wallpaper...

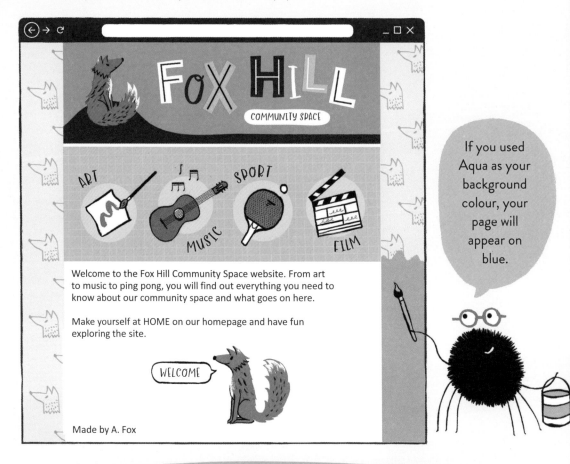

If you used Aqua as your background colour, your page will appear on blue.

INVISIBLE IMAGES

Most websites use images, but not everyone can see them – for example, if there is a slow connection and a picture won't load, if a picture isn't linked properly, or if a user is using a **screen reader**, a device that reads out content for users who are blind or visually impaired.

alt attributes help by giving alternative information for users who can't see images – they appear as text that is read by a user or screen reader.

For example, to set **alt attributes** for the images you've used so far, you could add:

```
<img src="images/banner.png" alt="Fox Hill banner">
<img src="images/header.png" alt="Activities at Fox Hill">
<img src="images/fox.png" alt="A fox saying 'welcome'">
```

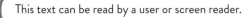

This text can be read by a user or screen reader.

DEBUGGING

If your web page doesn't come out the way you expected, you'll need to fix your code. This is known as **debugging**, because coding errors are known as **bugs**. The good thing about HTML and CSS is that even if there are errors, your website will still work – it just won't look the way you want it to.

In HTML and CSS, most errors are **syntax bugs**. 'Syntax' means the way the words are arranged. Syntax bugs happen when you haven't typed something correctly. Have a look at this example...

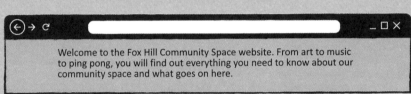

Welcome to the Fox Hill Community Space website. From art to music to ping pong, you will find out everything you need to know about our community space and what goes on here.

There is no white box behind the text. Look at this code to see why...

```
.middle (
    width: 45%;
    margin: auto;
    background: white;
}
```

This should be a curly bracket.

The browser won't recognise a CSS rule without the correct brackets, so it doesn't make a white box.

You can spot bugs by going back and checking your code CAREFULLY. It's a good habit to get into. ALL coders, however good, have to spend time debugging their code.

CHECKLIST

Here are some things to think about when debugging.

✓ **Punctuation** – have you used the right brackets? And separated CSS declarations with **;** ?

✓ **Spelling** – computers can't recognize misspelled words. Check your spelling.

✓ **Open tags and rules** – if you leave an HTML tag or CSS rule open, the computer won't know where it ends, so check all your tags and rules are closed.

✓ **Broken links** – this happens when the computer can't find something you've linked to, such as an image or another page. Check you've typed the link correctly and the file hasn't been moved.

STYLE SHEETS

CSS inside your HTML document is known an **internal style sheet**. As you add more pages to your site, it will be easier to use a separate file, or **external style sheet**. Then you can apply the same look to a new page just by copying and pasting a single link.

1. Start by creating a new document for your CSS. Open a new file in Notepad++ and save it as 'stylesheet.css'. The '.css' in the name tells Notepad++ you're writing a style sheet and everything inside it will be CSS.

2. Now to move the CSS you've already created into the new style sheet. Open your 'index.html' file.

Select all the CSS between the style tags by highlighting it. To do this, click and drag your mouse across the CSS – then press **Ctrl+X** to cut the highlighted section (see 'Handy Shortcuts', on the right).

In Notepad++, when you click on a tag or bracket, its matching tag or bracket is highlighted. This means you can see if one is missing or matched incorrectly.

```
body {
    background-image: url("images/bg.png");
    background-repeat: repeat;
    font-family: Calibri;
    font-size: 20px;
}

.middle {
    width: 45%;
    margin: auto;
    background: white;
}

section {
    width: 100%;
    padding-bottom: 10px;
}

section img {
    width: 100%;
}
```

I'm looking GOOOD.

3. Go back to 'stylesheet.css' and paste the CSS you cut by pressing **Ctrl+V**. Then save.

4. Now, you can now delete the **<style>** tags from the 'index.html' file.

```
<!DOCTYPE html>
<html>

<head>
  <meta charset="UTF-8">
  <title>Fox Hill Community Space</title>
  <style>
  </style>
</head>

<body>
```

Delete these.

5. Next, link your style sheet to your 'index.html' file. Type this after your title.

```
<title>Fox Hill Community Space</title>
<link href="stylesheet.css" rel="stylesheet">
```

The first part of the link says where the style sheet is. The second part tells the browser the link is for styling.

6. Save the updated 'index.html' file and run it in your browser. It should look exactly the same as before – but now you have a style sheet you can use to style new pages.

HANDY SHORTCUTS

Cut, **copy** and **paste** are so common they have their own keyboard shortcuts.

- To cut, select the text you want to move, then press **Ctrl+X**.
- To copy, select the text you want to copy, then press **Ctrl+C**.
- To paste, click where you want to paste what you've cut or copied, then press **Ctrl+V**.

Another useful shortcut is 'undo'. Press **Ctrl+Z** and the last thing you did will be undone. This is helpful if you make a mistake.

STYLE ANOTHER PAGE

1. You can now style your links page. Open your 'links.html' file and add the style sheet link to the head, like this.

```
<!DOCTYPE html>
<html>

<head>
  <meta charset="UTF-8">
  <title> Fox Hill Links </title>
  <link href="stylesheet.css" rel="stylesheet">
</head>

<body>
  <section>
    <a href="index.html"><img src="images/banner.png" alt="Fox Hill banner"></a>
    <p>Here are links to websites recommended by Fox Hill Community Space.</p>
    <a href="https://usborne.com/">Click here to find out where Fox Hill
    Community Space gets the books for their library...</a>
```

This links to your style sheet.

2. You'll need to add a white box for the text on the links page, too. The CSS for the box is already in your style sheet, but you need to tell the browser where the box goes. Open and close **<div>** tags around all the text – just as you did on your homepage.

*The **<div>** class must be 'middle' to match your style sheet.*

```
<body>
  <div class="middle">
    <section>
      <p>Here are links to websites recommended by Fox Hill Community Space.</p>
      <a href="https://usborne.com/">Click here to find out where Fox Hill
      Community Space gets the books for their library...</a>
      <br>
      <a href="https://www.youtube.com/user/UsbornePublishing">Click here to
      watch some GROOVY videos...</a>
      <br>
      <a href="https://www.usborne.com/quicklinks/">This is a link to a site
      full of links...</a>
    </section>
    <footer>Made by A. Fox</footer>
  </div>
</body>
```

Everything between these tags will be in the white box.

3. Save and run the links page in your browser. The style should now match the style of your homepage.

Here are links to websites recommended by Fox Hill Community Space.

Click here to find out where Fox Hill Community Space gets the books for their library...
Click here to watch some GROOVY videos...
This is a link to a site full of links...

Made by A. Fox

The text you click on to go to a link is known as **anchor text**. **Search engines** – meaning websites that search for other websites – look at ALL the text on a page when searching. But, if there is a match in the anchor text, the search engine puts the site nearer the top of its results.

UNDERLINED LINKS

Links are automatically underlined. If you DON'T want underlined links, you can add this rule to your style sheet.

```
a {
   text-decoration: none;
}
```

This is useful if you're using IMAGES as links – without it the images will have a tiny line under them.

FANCY FONTS

So far you've used **web-safe fonts** – the basic fonts all computers have. However you can use any font you like, as long as you link to it. Here's how.

1. Some fonts have to be paid for, but there are plenty of free ones available on websites. Just search for 'free fonts' online. When you find a font you like, you should also see a link to copy and paste.

You can find out more about free fonts and where to find them by going to Usborne Quicklinks.

2. Font links go between the **<head>** tags in the HTML file for the page. Open your 'links.html' file and add the following link under your style sheet link. Then save.

```
<title>Fox Hill Links</title>
<link href="style sheet.css" rel="stylesheet">
<link href="https://fonts.googleapis.com/
css?family=Neucha&display=swap" rel="stylesheet">
```

This is the link provided by the font website. To use another font, just change the link.

3. Now open your 'stylesheet.css' file and change the 'font family' to your new font.

```
font-family: Neucha, cursive;
font-size: 20px;
}
```

'Cursive' means the font looks a bit like handwriting.

FANCY FONT   FANCY FONT   FANCY FONT

4. Run your 'links.html' file in your browser.
You should see the new font.

BACK-UP FONTS

When using fancy fonts, it's a good idea to list a web-safe font such as 'Calibri' as a back-up in case anything goes wrong (for example, if the font website updates its links).

> The browser will try to use the first font. If it can't find it, it will use the next one in your list – known as a **font stack**.

> Each **font family** starts with a capital letter.

```
font-family: Neucha, cursive, Calibri;
```

> If you DON'T want to use your new font on some pages, don't add the link and the browser will use the font you started with.

WARNING!

You can't add links to style sheets – so you'll need to link to your new font in the HTML for every page.

MAKING TABLES

Tables display information or **data** in rows and columns – for example in a timetable. This makes it easy to compare and look things up. HTML has tags especially for making tables. Here's how to create a 'What's On' page with a timetable.

HOW TO MAKE A TABLE

1. Open your template in Notepad++ and save it as 'whatson.html'.
Add links to your stylesheet and font in the **<head>**, like this.

```
<head>
  <meta charset="UTF-8">
  <title>What's On</title>
  <link href="stylesheet.css" rel="stylesheet">
  <link href="https://fonts.googleapis.com/
css?family=Neucha&display=swap" rel="stylesheet">
```

2. Now divide your page for styling and add your banner. After your opening tags, add this.

```
<body>
  <div class="middle">
   <section>
    <a href="home.html"><img src="images/banner.png" alt="Fox Hill banner"></a>
```

3. Add a paragraph to introduce the table.

```
    <p>Have a look at what's on at Fox Hill Community Space this week.</p>
```

4. Now to create a timetable with three columns.
Type this to create the column headings.

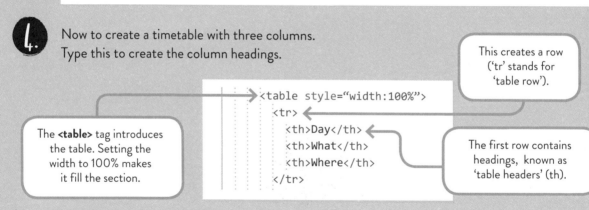

This creates a row ('tr' stands for 'table row').

```
<table style="width:100%">
  <tr>
   <th>Day</th>
   <th>What</th>
   <th>Where</th>
  </tr>
```

The **<table>** tag introduces the table. Setting the width to 100% makes it fill the section.

The first row contains headings, known as 'table headers' (th).

5. Then, add your first row of entries, one for each column.

```
<tr>
  <td>Monday</td>
  <td>Printmaking</td>
  <td>The Art Room</td>
</tr>
```

<td> or 'table data' tags go around the content for each column.

6. Each row needs a pair of **<tr>** tags, and its own set of **<td>** tags. Type this to fill out the table. Then close your **<table>** tags.

```
<tr>
  <td>Tuesday</td>
  <td>Drama</td>
  <td>The Studio</td>
</tr>
<tr>
  <td>Wednesday</td>
  <td>Coding Club</td>
  <td>Room 5</td>
</tr>
<tr>
  <td>Thursday</td>
  <td>Jazz Choir</td>
  <td>The Studio</td>
</tr>
<tr>
  <td>Friday</td>
  <td>Open Mic</td>
  <td>The Cafe</td>
</tr>
<tr>
  <td>Saturday</td>
  <td>Dancing</td>
  <td>The Hall</td>
</tr>
<tr>
  <td>Sunday</td>
  <td>Drawing</td>
  <td>The Art Room</td>
</tr>
</table>
```

6. Close your **<section>** tags and add a footer.
Then close all your open tags.

```
      </table>
    </section>
    <footer>Made by A. Fox</footer>
  </div>
</body>

</html>
```

7. Save the page and run it in your browser.
It should look something like this...

Well! All the information is there,
but it could look neater. Read on to style
your table using CSS .

34

TIDY TABLE

1. Open up 'stylesheet.css' and type the following rule...

```
table, td, th {
  text-align: left;
}
```

This puts ALL the text on the left.

You can make the same rule apply to different elements by separating each one with a comma.

You can add a border to your table if you want. Just add an extra property to your table rule.

```
border: 1px solid black;

border-collapse: collapse;
```

Without 'collapse', there would be separate borders around every entry in the table.

2. Next, add this rule to give every even row a background colour.

We chose LightSeaGreen to match the banner, but you can use any colour you want.

```
tr:nth-child(even) {
  background-color: LightSeaGreen;
}
```

OrangeRed

LightSeaGreen

PeachPuff

ForestGreen

3. Save your style sheet, go back to 'whatson.html' and run your page again. Now your table should look like this...

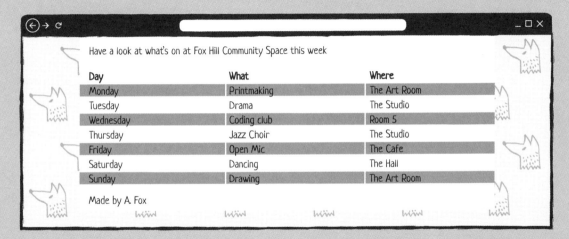

Have a look at what's on at Fox Hill Community Space this week

Day	What	Where
Monday	Printmaking	The Art Room
Tuesday	Drama	The Studio
Wednesday	Coding club	Room 5
Thursday	Jazz Choir	The Studio
Friday	Open Mic	The Cafe
Saturday	Dancing	The Hall
Sunday	Drawing	The Art Room

Made by A. Fox

ADDING VIDEOS

If you want to include videos or other big files on your website,
it's best just to provide a link to a source elsewhere on the internet.
This is known as **embedding** – and it means you don't have to
worry about big files overloading your site.

1. Start by making a new page for your videos.
Open your template and save it as 'videos.html'.

2. Add a link to your style sheet in the head.

```
<!DOCTYPE html>
<html lang="en">

<head>
  <meta charset="UTF-8">
  <title>Videos</title>
  <link href="stylesheet.css" rel="stylesheet">
  <link href="https://fonts.googleapis.com/css?
  family=Neucha" rel="stylesheet">
</head>
```

3. Then, add opening **\<div\>** and **\<section\>** tags to
contain a text box, the Fox Hill banner and an
introduction to your new page.

```
<body>
  <div class="middle">
    <section>
      <a href="home.html"><img src="images/banner.png" alt="Fox Hill banner"></a>
      <p>Here is a video from the Fox Hill Cinemaniacs showing you how to
      make an origami fox.</p>
```

Your introduction goes between
the paragraph **\<p\>** tags.

4. Embedded files need a frame to appear in. You create a frame using **<iFrame>** tags. Type the following.

> These set the size of the frame.

```
<iframe width="560" height="315" src="https://www.youtube.com/embed/
BhzmnC9j3EE" frameborder="0" allow="accelerometer; autoplay; encrypted-
media; gyroscope; picture-in-picture" allowfullscreen></iframe>
```

This is the link to the video you're embedding. To embed a different file, just replace the link.

The quickest way to embed files is usually just to copy and paste the link directly from a website (see box).

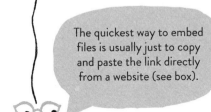

FILES TO SHARE

Lots of sites share or **host** videos. Most sites that allow sharing have an option to 'share'. You just click on the option and then choose **Embed**. Clicking on **Embed** will give you a tag containing the link to copy and paste into the HTML.

5. Finish your page by adding a footer and closing your tags, and save the whole page.

```
    </section>
    <footer>Made by A. Fox</footer>
   </div>
</body>

</html>
```

SHARING

When you embed a video from another website, that site is responsible for online copyright – a law that gives the person who created or owns something the right to decide who can use it.

However you should ALWAYS be careful what you share. Only share files visitors to your site will be happy to see, and always credit your original source.

6. Adding a video pushes your footer into the wrong place. To fix that, open 'stylesheet.css' and type the following.

```
footer {
  width: 50%;
  padding: 8px;
  margin: auto;
}
```

This styles the space around the Fox Hill footer.

7. Save your style sheet and go back to your video page. Save it and run your new page in your browser. It should look something like this...

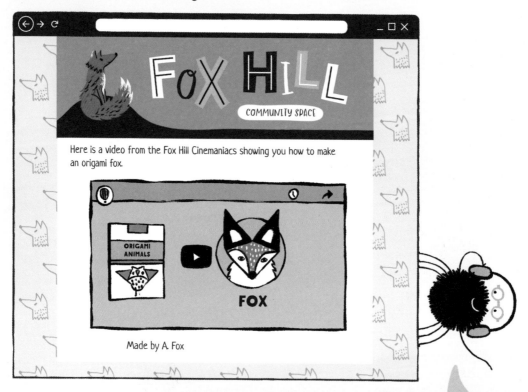

If you want to include your OWN videos, music or games on a web page, the easiest way is to upload them to a sharing site. Then you can embed them in the way you've just done.

ADDING A MAP

You can use an **<iframe>** tag to embed ANY kind of document. All you have to do is copy and paste the tag from the website. Here's how to find and embed an online map.

1. Open the HTML file for the page where you want the map. Open your browser and go to a map website. Search for the place you're looking for and you should see something like this...

Directions   Nearby   Send   Share

2. Click on **Share** and a window like this
will pop up. Click on **Embed a map**.

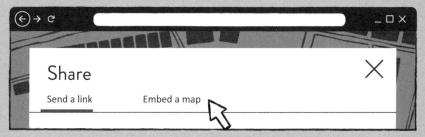

3. You should now see an **<iframe>** tag.
Click on **COPY HTML** and the
entire tag will be copied.

> This part of the tag
> will be different every
> time, depending
> on what you're
> embedding and
> where it's from.

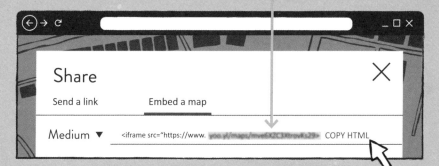

4. Paste the tag into the part of the HTML file where you want the map to
appear. Save and run your file. You should now see something like this.

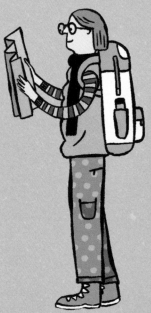

MINI ANIMATIONS

Using CSS you can combine two images to make a moving picture or mini **animation** on your homepage.

To start with, you can animate the fox you've already got on your homepage. Your mini animation will fade between two nearly identical images, so they appear to move.

1. Open your 'index.html' file in Notepad++. After the text, you're going to add two images to make an animation using images from Quicklinks. You also need to give both images a new class and wrap them in **<div>** tags. Delete the fox image link, then type this before your closing **<section>** tag.

> **Animations** work by moving quickly through a sequence of images. This tricks your eye into thinking it is seeing movement.

Delete this line.

This is the first image.

```
<a href="links.html"><img src="images/fox.png"></a>
<div class="animation">
  <img class="bottom" src="images/fox.png" alt="Fox waving tail">
  <img class="top" src="images/fox2.png" alt="Fox waving tail">
</div>
</section>
```

This is the second image.

This **<div>** tag keeps the images tidy inside your page. 'animation' is to work with in CSS.

Adding a **class** means you can work with JUST these images in the style sheet. If you don't add a class, your CSS rule would apply to ALL images.

2. That's all you need to do in this file, so save it and open your 'stylesheet.css' file. Type in the following to position both images, using the 'animation' class.

```
.animation {
  position: relative;
  margin: 0 auto;
}
```

These create a neat space in the middle of your page for your image.

3. Now add a rule to position the 'bottom' image in the **<div>** box.

```
.bottom {
  position: absolute;
}
```

absolute means the image automatically appears in the top left corner of the **<div>** box that it's in.

4. Now, add a rule for the 'top' image. You are going to use five selectors to set how this image appears. Type the following.

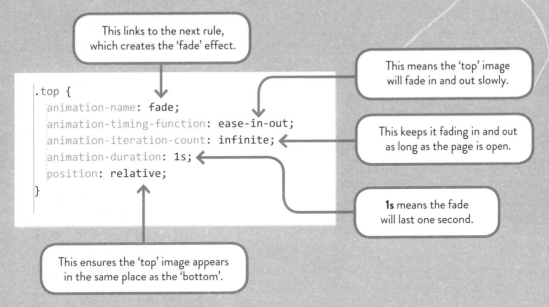

This links to the next rule, which creates the 'fade' effect.

This means the 'top' image will fade in and out slowly.

This keeps it fading in and out as long as the page is open.

```
.top {
  animation-name: fade;
  animation-timing-function: ease-in-out;
  animation-iteration-count: infinite;
  animation-duration: 1s;
  position: relative;
}
```

1s means the fade will last one second.

This ensures the 'top' image appears in the same place as the 'bottom'.

5. Finally, you need to add a rule to style the animation. This rule will apply to the CSS itself, rather than the HTML, so you will need a special kind of rule known as an **at-rule**.

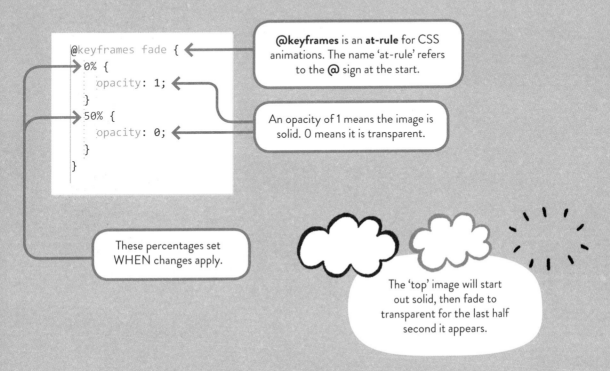

@keyframes is an **at-rule** for CSS animations. The name 'at-rule' refers to the **@** sign at the start.

```
@keyframes fade {
  0% {
    opacity: 1;
  }
  50% {
    opacity: 0;
  }
}
```

An opacity of 1 means the image is solid. 0 means it is transparent.

These percentages set WHEN changes apply.

The 'top' image will start out solid, then fade to transparent for the last half second it appears.

6. Save and close your CSS file, and go back to 'index.html'. Run the page in your browser. If you used our images, the fox should look like it's waving its tail.

USING YOUR OWN PICTURES

You can easily replace the images to create your own animation. You just need two versions of your chosen image – to show before and after the movement.

1. Create two images to use.
- You can use photographs if you take a before and after shot.
- You can create pictures on your computer, using an image-editing or drawing program such as **Microsoft® Paint**.
- You can draw images on paper and then photograph them.

2. Whatever kind of images you use, make sure they're saved as image files ('jpeg' or 'png'). Photos on a phone or digital camera are usually saved automatically as 'jpegs'.

3. Then, transfer the images to your computer. If you took photographs on a smartphone, you can email them to yourself, open the email on your computer and save the images from the email to your 'Images' folder.

4. For the animation to work smoothly, the images need to be exactly the same size. Check the sizes by going to your images folder and clicking once on each image. The dimensions appear at the bottom of the folder window.

Image size is measured in **pixels** (px) - the tiny dots that make up a screen. Usually, the larger the number of pixels, the bigger the image.

about-button	Status: 👥 Shared	Dimensions: 68 x 28
PNG image	Date taken: 22/01/2019 15:04	Size: 10.8 KB

42

If the images have different dimensions, you will need to resize one. For this, you also need an image-editing program. Our instructions use Microsoft® Paint, but most image-editing programs work in a similar way.

RESIZING PICTURES

1. Open Microsoft® Paint by clicking on the 'Start Menu' icon, then **All Programs** and then **Accessories**. Double-click on Microsoft® Paint.

2. Click on the file image in the Microsoft® Paint toolbar and choose **Open** to open your image file. Then click on **Resize** in the toolbar. Click on **Pixels** and make sure **Maintain aspect ratio** is checked. Then change the numbers to match the image size you want.

You can also resize images using an image-resizing website. Go to Usborne Quicklinks to find out more.

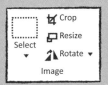

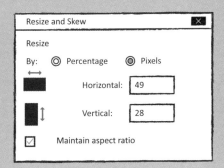

3. Click **OK** and save your file.

CREATE YOUR ANIMATION

To create your animation, go back to your HTML file and replace the image names with the names of your new pictures. Save and run your page to see your new animation.

```
<div class="animation">
  <img class="bottom" src="images/newpic.jpg">
  <img class="top" src="images/newpic2.jpg">
</div>
```

WHAT'S ON THE MENU?

Now you have a few different pages, you need a way of getting between them. This means creating a menu bar.

1. You're going to create a menu with images that you can click on to go to different pages. You can do this with list tags. Open your 'index.html' file and add the following after the **<img>** tag for your banner.

LISTS

A list is a way of organizing information, by putting one item after another in a... list.
<ul> tags create lists with bullet points.
<ol> tags create lists with numbers.

This tells the browser you're making a list.

Setting the class as 'menu' means you will ONLY be styling the menu bar, so you can use list tags elsewhere without having to rewrite your style sheet.

<li> stands for 'list item'.

Each 'list item' contains a link followed by an image tag. This means when you click on the image, it will take you to the page in the link.

Each page needs its own list entry. To add another page to your site, just add another entry before your closing **<ul>** tag.

```
<section>
    <img src="images/banner.png" alt="Fox
    Hill banner">
    <ul class="menu">
        <li>
            <a href="videos.html"><img
            src="images/videos.png"></a>
        </li>
        <li>
            <a href="links.html"><img
            src="images/links.png"></a>
        </li>
        <li>
            <a href="whatson.html"><img
            src="images/whatson.png">
            </a>
        </li>
    </ul>
```

2. To make the menu bar appear on each page, you need to add the code for it to each HTML file. Select the **<ul>** tags and everything in between, and use **Ctrl+C** to copy them. Then use **Ctrl+V** to paste them into each file after the **<img>** tag for your banner.

3. Now, adjust the layout of your homepage to keep everything tidy below the menu bar. Go back to your homepage and add another **<div>** tag, like this.

> This tag goes around the content inside your **<section>** tags.

```
<img src="images/header.png" alt="Activities at Fox Hill">
<div class="innersection">
  <p>Welcome to the Fox Hill Community Space website. From art
  to music to ping pong, you will find out everything you need
  to know about our community space and what goes on here.</p>
  <p>Make yourself at HOME on our homepage and have fun exploring
  the site. </p>
</div>
<div class="animation">
  <img class="bottom" src="images/fox.png" alt="Fox waving tail">
  <img class="top" src="images/fox2.png" alt="Fox waving tail">
</div>
</section>
```

Links

What's on

MENU

Videos

45

4. Save your homepage. Then open your style sheet so you can style your new menu. First, you need to style the 'innersection' – the content you just put a **<div>** tag around.

```
.innersection {
  width: 70%;
  margin: auto;
}
```

LOOKING AT CODE

If you want to look at the code of ANY website, there is an easy way. On the menu bar at the top of any browser, click on the **Tools** tab and then the **Developer** tool. This will show you all the code for the website.

5. Now to set the style of the menu bar. Type in the following.

'none' means the list will have no numbers or bullet points.

```
ul {
  list-style-type: none;
  display: flex;
  justify-content: center;
  padding: 0px;
  margin: 0px;
}
```

This makes your menu bar expand or shrink to fit the screen.

This puts the content in the middle. It's spelled 'center' because HTML and CSS use US spelling.

6. You also need a rule for the menu itself. This will set the width of the list entries (that is the pictures and text) inside it. Add the following to your style sheet and save it.

```
li {
  width: 20%;
}
```

MENU

⌘❍ Links

▷ Videos

? What's on

7. Go back to your homepage and run it.
It should now look like this.

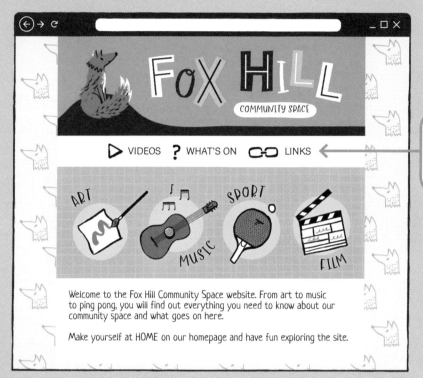

When you click on the menu bar images, you should be taken to the other pages on your site.

HAVING PROBLEMS?

If your homepage doesn't look quite right, check the debugging tips on page 25 carefully. If that doesn't reveal what's wrong, you can use an online validator or validation website to check your code. Go to Quicklinks for some recommended links.

1. Open the validation website in your browser.

2. Upload your HTML or CSS file by clicking **Browse** and selecting your file.

Validate by File Upload

Upload a document for validation:

File: [Browse...] No file selected.

3. The validator will check the code line by line, highlighting any problems with suggestions for fixing them.

PLAYING WITH LAYOUT

It's easy to tweak the layout of your homepage.
Here are a couple of things to try.

BIGGER BANNER

Your website already has a banner, but you
can change your code to make it BIGGER.

1. First, you need to add a rule for your
banner. Open your style sheet and type
this after your last rule. Then save your file.

```
.banner {
  width: 100%;
  display: block;
  margin-left: auto;
  margin-right: auto;
}
```

> This will make the banner fill the entire width of the screen.

2. Now open your 'index.html' file. After your
opening **<body>** tag, add a new **<div>** tag like this.

> This links to the CSS rule you just added.

```
<body>
  <div>
    <img class="banner" src="images/banner.png"
    alt="Fox Hill banner">
  </div>
```

3. Finally, delete the original **<img>** tag for
the banner highlighted below.

```
  <section>
    <img src="images/banner.png" alt="Fox Hill banner">
    <ul class="menu">
```

DESIGN TIPS

You can think about web page
design as an inverted pyramid.

VERY important stuff

Some other stuff

Things I don't
really care if
you read.

Your most important information
goes at the top. This is your
banner. It should be BIG.

Useful but less important
information goes in the middle.
This should be medium-sized.

Finally, in small print, at the
bottom, is the least important
information. Not everyone will
read it, but it's there if they want
to check. This is your footer.

Now run the page in your browser. You should see something like this...

Your banner should stretch right across your screen.

MENU ON THE SIDE

You can also make your menu options appear down the side of the page, instead of across the top. The following makes a side menu where each item is a bar that slides in from the side of the page when your mouse hovers over it.

1. Open your 'index.html' file and save a new copy as 'sidemenuindex.html'.

2. Highlight and delete your old menu bar (everything between your **<ul>** tags).

```
<ul class="menu">
  <li>
    <a href="videos.html"><img
    src="images/videos.png"></a>
  </li>
  <li>
    <a href="links.html"><img
    src="images/links.png"></a>
  </li>
  <li>
    <a href="whatson.html"><img
    src="images/whatson.png">
    </a>
  </li>
</ul>
```

Only the tip of each bar is visible until it slides inwards.

49

3. Now to create your new menu bar. This goes inside a **<div>** tag, with each page link inside its own **<a>** tag. Type the following where the **<ul>** tags used to be.

```
<div class="sidenav">
<a href="links.html" class="links">Links</a>
<a href="whatson.html" class="whatson">What's On</a>
<a href="videos.html" class="videos">Videos</a>
</div>
```

Each **<a>** tag contains the address of the link, its class for styling and the text that will appear on the bar.

STYLE YOUR NEW MENU

1. Open your style sheet and add this rule for the bars.

```
.sidenav a {
  position: absolute;
  left: -150px;
  transition: 0.3s;
  padding: 15px;
  width: 150px;
  text-decoration: none;
  font-size: 20px;
  color: white;
}
```

This positions the left edge of each bar 150 pixels to the left of the page.

This means when the mouse hovers over a bar, it will take 0.3 seconds to change.

2. To make each bar react to the mouse hovering on it, type this.

```
.sidenav a:hover {
  left: 0;
}
```

This moves the bar across so the whole bar appears on the page.

3. As the bars will need to be positioned below each other, they need individual rules. You can give them different colours when you do this (we chose colours to match the rest of the page). Type the following and save.

```
.videos {
  top: 20px;
  background-color: DarkCyan;
}

.whatson {
  top: 80px;
  background-color: Orange;
}

.links {
  top: 140px;
  background-color: Firebrick;
}
```

This is the distance from the top, in pixels.

4. Go back to your 'sidemenuindex.html' file and run the page in your browser. Your page should now look like the picture below.

COLOUR TIPS

Too many colours can make a website look too busy. It's a good idea to stick to no more than three main colours, plus neutral shades such as grey or lighter shades of your main colour(s).

If you hover your mouse over a bar, it should slide out. You can click on it to go to that page.

JavaScript

In this section you will find out how to make your website do more with JavaScript. So far you've used HTML, a markup language, and CSS, a style-sheet language. But, JavaScript is a little different, because it's a **programming language** – meaning it's designed for writing **programs** or complete sets of instructions for computers. Coders use JavaScript to write mini programs, known as **scripts**, for web pages.

WELCOME!

Now you've made a basic website, you can add JavaScript to make it interactive – so it can react to visitors.

Your first bit of JavaScript will welcome visitors to your site. You do this by adding a pop-up window known as an **alert box** to your homepage.

1. Open your 'index.html' page. Create an alert box by adding the following before your closing **<body>** tag.

> **<script>** tags tell the browser you're about to use JavaScript.

> This tells the browser to create an alert box when the page loads. Whatever you type between the " " will appear in the box.

```
<script>
  alert( "Welcome to Fox Hill!" );
</script>
</body>
```

SCRIPT TAGS

JavaScript **<script>** tags can go between the **<head>** tags OR **<body>** tags in your HTML file. Browsers load code in the order it appears, so many coders put **<script>** tags before the last **<body>** tag. This means browsers can load the rest of the page first.

2. Now save and run your page. You should see something like this.

> When you click on the **OK** button, the box will disappear.

SLIDESHOW

You can also use JavaScript to make parts of a page move and change. This means you can create a slideshow which automatically changes the pictures on display.

As well as a new page for the slideshow, you're going to make more new pages later. So you can save time by creating a new page template.

MAKE A NEW PAGE TEMPLATE

1. Open 'index.html' and save a copy as 'newtemplate.html'.

2. Delete your script and everything between the menu and the closing **<section>** tag.

3. Save again and your new template is ready to use. Your template should look like this...

The template contains links to your style sheet, banner and menu bar, so you can quickly make new pages that look the same.

```
<!DOCTYPE html>
<html lang="en">

<head>
    <meta charset="UTF-8">
    <title>Fox Hill Community Space</title>
    <link rel="styleheet" href="stylesheet.css">
    <link rel="stylesheet" href="https://fonts.googleapis.com/
    css?family=Neucha">
</head>

<body>
  <div class="middle">
    <section>
        <a href="index.html"><img src="images/banner.png"
        alt="Fox Hill banner"></a>
        <ul class="menu">
          <li>
            <a href="videos.html"><img src="images/videos.png" alt=
            "Videos"></a>
          </li>
          <li>
            <a href="links.html"><img src="images/links.png"
            alt="Links"></a>
          </li>
          <li>
            <a href="whatson.html"><img src="images/whatson.png"
            alt="What's on"></a>
          </li>
          </ul>
    </section>
    <footer>Made by A. Fox</footer>
    </div>
</body>

</html>
```

This is the finished template.

To give your pages different names, just change the title each time you use the template.

SET UP YOUR PICTURES

1. Open 'newtemplate.html' and save a copy as 'pictures.html'.

2. Next you need to add the pictures, putting each one inside a **<div>** tag. For the first picture, type the following after your menu.

> This is the picture you're linking to.

> This labels the order of the pictures.

```
<div class="slideshow">
    <div class="numbertext">1 / 3</div>
    <img src="images/img1.jpg" alt="Painting">
    <div class="text">Painting at the studio</div>
</div>
```

> Each picture will have a **<div>** tag wrapped around 3 more tags.

> This adds a caption underneath the picture.

3. Do the same for the rest of your pictures. We've added two more, but you can include as many as you like.

```
<div class="slideshow">
    <div class="numbertext">2 / 3</div>
    <img src="images/img2.jpg" alt="Coding club">
    <div class="text">Coding club</div>
</div>
<div class="slideshow">
    <div class="numbertext">3 / 3</div>
    <img src="images/img3.jpg" alt="Dancing">
    <div class="text">Dancing</div>
</div>
```

> This is for the second picture.

> This is for the third picture.

Now you can begin the JavaScript for the slideshow itself. This will mean writing a short program known as a **function** (see right).

FUNCTIONS

A **function** is a short program that does a particular job – such as display a slideshow. Each function has its own name, which you **call** to make it run. The whole function goes between curly brackets: **{ }**.

CREATE YOUR SLIDESHOW

1. Tell the browser you're going to use JavaScript by opening a **<script>** tag between your closing 'middle' **<div>** and **<body>** tags.

```
    </div>
    <script>
</body>
```

2. Next you need to organize your pictures using a **variable** (see box). We've called it 'pictureIndex'.

```
    var pictureIndex = 0;
```

This sets the starting value of the variable to zero. In JavaScript, complete lines, known as **statements**, are separated by semicolons **;** .

This creates a variable named 'pictureIndex'. It's set in another two spaces, because it's inside the **<script>** tags.

3. Tell the browser to **call** or run the **function** you're going to write in step 4.

```
    showPics();
```

This is the function.

4. Now, you need to create the **function** itself. Open the **function** and set up a couple of variables, like this.

This curly bracket marks the start of the function. Everything inside the function is set in another two spaces.

'i' stands for a number.

```
    function showPics() {
      var i;
      var pictures = document.getElementsByClassName("slideshow");
```

'pictures' means everything inside **<div>** tags with the class 'slideshow'.

These lines create two more variables inside the function.

CAMEL CASE

JavaScript doesn't allow hyphens or spaces in names – so coders use **camel case** instead. This means closing up gaps and putting capital letters in the middle of words (making them look bumpy, like camel humps). So 'Java script' becomes 'JavaScript', for example.

VARIABLES

A **variable** is like a box with a label. You can store different things or **values** in it, without changing the label.

5. Then use those variables to tell the computer how long to display each picture. You do this with a repeating chunk of code known as a **loop**.

FOR

IF

LOOPS

Loops repeat a block of code until a certain condition is met. They often begin with FOR, IF or WHILE. A **FOR** loop will run AS LONG AS that statement is true. An **IF** loop will only run IF it is true. **WHILE** loops run WHILE it is true.

```
for (i = 0; i < pictures.length; i++) {
  pictures[i].style.display = "none";
}
```

The loop will run until **i** is greater than 'pictures.length' (the number of elements named 'pictures').

++ adds 1 to the value each time the loop runs.

This means that IF the pictures meet the **FOR** conditions they WON'T be displayed. This line is indented inside the loop.

6. To finish the function, you need another loop to tell the browser how long to show each picture and what to do when all the pictures have been shown. Type this and close your **<script>** tags.

If 'pictureIndex' becomes bigger than 'pictures', its value goes back to 1 – and the pictures start showing from the beginning again.

```
pictureIndex++;
if (pictureIndex > pictures.length) {
  pictureIndex = 1
}
pictures[pictureIndex-1].style.display = "block";
setTimeout(showPics, 2000);
}
</script>
```

This tells the browser which picture to display.

2000 makes the picture show for two seconds. The bigger the number, the longer it will show.

7. The finished JavaScript should look like this. Save and run your page.

NESTING JAVASCRIPT

JavaScript is easier to read if you **nest** it in the same way as you nest tags in HTML. Each dotted column in our code represents two spaces.

```
<script>
  var pictureIndex = 0;
  showPics();

  function showPics() {
    var i;
    var pictures = document.getElementsByClassName("slideshow");
    for (i = 0; i < pictures.length; i++) {
      pictures[i].style.display = "none";
    }
    pictureIndex++;
    if (pictureIndex > pictures.length) {
      pictureIndex = 1
    }
    pictures[pictureIndex-1].style.display = "block";
    setTimeout(showPics, 2000);
  }
</script>
```

The spacing makes it easy to see which lines belong inside the function.

The code that runs in a loop is set in another two spaces.

The curly brackets **{ }** frame functions and other complete bits of code.

You should see your new slideshow appear under your menu bar, with the pictures changing every 2 seconds.

COMMUNITY SPACE

▷ VIDEOS   ? WHAT'S ON   ∞ LINKS

1 / 3

Painting at the studio
Made by A. Fox

ADDING DOTS AND ARROWS

So far, the pictures in the slideshow change automatically. With a little more code, you can add clickable arrows to move backwards and forwards, and dots to go straight to a picture. For the arrows, you'll need to use **numeric code** (see box on the right).

1. Start by wrapping a new **<div>** tag with the class 'slideshow-container' around the three 'slideshow' **<div>** tags.

```
<div class="slideshow-container">
<div class="slideshow">
  <div class="numbertext">1 / 3</div>
  <img src="image/img1.jpg" alt="Painting">
  <div class="text">Painting at the studio</div>
</div>
<div class="slideshow">
  <div class="numbertext">2 / 3</div>
  <img src="image/img2.jpg" alt="Coding">
  <div class="text">Coding club</div>
</div>
<div class="slideshow">
  <div class="numbertext">3 / 3</div>
  <img src="image/img3.jpg" alt="Dancing">
  <div class="text">Dancing</div>
</div>
</div>
```

2. Now to add arrow buttons on either side of each picture. Type this before the closing 'slideshow-container' **<div>** tag.

```
</div>
<a class="prev" onclick="nextPicture(-1)">&#10094;</a>
<a class="next" onclick="nextPicture(1)">&#10095;</a>
</div>
```

This is your closing **<div>** tag with the class 'middle'.

onclick is an **attribute** – it makes programs run when you click on something.

This will be the name of a JavaScript function that moves through the pictures. You'll create it in step 5.

This is a LEFT arrow in numeric code.

This is a RIGHT arrow in numeric code.

NUMERIC CODE

Numeric code is a way of encoding letters and symbols. Each letter, number or symbol has its own code, which any computer anywhere will recognize.

It's mostly used to encode symbols or letters that aren't on your keyboard – for example, **Ⓒ** is © .

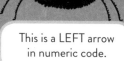

3. For the dots, you'll need some more **<div>** tags. Type this below the tags for your arrows.

> This positions three 'dots' below the middle of each picture.

```
<div style="text-align:center">
  <div class="dot" onclick="currentPicture(1)"></div>
  <div class="dot" onclick="currentPicture(2)"></div>
  <div class="dot" onclick="currentPicture(3)"></div>
</div>
```

> Each dot has its own 'onclick' attribute to make it clickable.

> 'currentPicture' is a function you're going to write in Step 5.

4. Go back to the JavaScript between your **<script>** tags. On the first line, change the '0' to a '1' and add 'pictureIndex' after 'showPics', like this.

```
<script>
  var pictureIndex = 1;
  showPics(pictureIndex);
```

> This makes the function **showPics** run using the variable **pictureIndex**, which represents the total number of pictures.

> Do you mind if I post a picture of #@$%^J77$ on my website?

> Well, you should really ask HER.

PERMISSION FOR PICTURES

Pictures on the internet can be seen – and copied – by anyone. And once something is on the internet, you may not be able to control what happens to it. So, when you're choosing pictures, make sure you check who is in it and if you have their permission to share it. If you don't, or if it's not something you want everyone to see, don't put it online.

5. The interactive buttons need a few more JavaScript functions. Type the following after the code you just added.

n stands for a number. Here it is the value of **nextPicture** from step 2.

This is the function for your arrows. It allows you to move through the pictures in order by clicking an arrow.

Here **n** is the value of **currentPicture** from Step 3.

```javascript
function nextPicture(n) {
  showPics(pictureIndex +=n);
}

function currentPicture(n) {
  showPics(pictureIndex = n);
}
```

This is the function for your dots. It allows you to select a picture by clicking a dot.

6. You also need to adapt your **showPics** function, so the arrows and dots can control which picture is showing. Add an 'n' in the brackets after 'showPics'. Then add the extra code highlighted yellow.

This links the dots to the **<div>** tags in your HTML.

```javascript
function showPics(n) {
  var i;
  var pictures = document.getElementsByClassName("slideshow");
  var dots = document.getElementsByClassName("dot");
  if (n > pictures.length) {
    pictureIndex = 1
  }
  if (n < 1) {
    pictureIndex = pictures.length
  }
  for (i = 0; i < pictures.length; i++) {
    pictures[i].style.display = "none";
  }
```

These loops means that if you try to go beyond the last picture, you'll go back to the first, and vice versa.

7. Finally, add a FOR loop to make a dot 'active' when it is selected. You can then make the active dot change colour using your style sheet. Type in the yellow code and delete the pink.

```javascript
  pictureIndex++;
  if (pictureIndex > pictures.length) {
    pictureIndex = 1
  }
  for (i = 0; i < dots.length; i++) {
    dots[i].className = dots[i].className.replace(" active", "");
  }
  pictures[pictureIndex-1].style.display = "block";
  setTimeout(showPics, 2000);
  dots[pictureIndex-1].className += " active";
}
</script>
```

This selects the dot.

This makes the dot change back when not selected.

Your finished JavaScript should look like this. Check and save your file.

```javascript
var pictureIndex = 1;
showPics(pictureIndex);

function nextPicture(n) {
  showPics(pictureIndex += n);
}

function currentPicture(n) {
  showPics(pictureIndex = n);
}

function showPics(n) {
  var i;
  var pictures = document.getElementsByClassName("slideshow");
  var dots = document.getElementsByClassName("dot");
  if (n > pictures.length) {
    pictureIndex = 1
  }
  if (n < 1) {
    pictureIndex = pictures.length
  }
  for (i = 0; i < pictures.length; i++) {
    pictures[i].style.display = "none";
  }
  for (i = 0; i < dots.length; i++) {
    dots[i].className = dots[i].className.replace(" active", "");
  }
  pictures[pictureIndex-1].style.display = "block";
  dots[pictureIndex-1].className += " active";
}
```

> Remember to leave a space here – to the computer the space represents the dot being replaced by an active one.

STYLING THE SLIDESHOW

1. Before you run your page, you need to style it. Open 'stylesheet.css' and type this rule for the space in which the pictures appear.

```css
.slideshow-container {
  max-width: 1000px;
  position: relative;
  margin: auto;
}
```

> This means however large your image, it will never be wider than 1,000 pixels.

RULES

Rule 5

Rule 3

Rule 1

> Remember, style sheet rules are applied all at once – so it doesn't usually matter what order they go in.

63

2. The next rule is for your arrows. Type this.

```
.prev, .next {
  position: absolute;
  top: 50%;
  width: auto;
  padding: 16px;
  color: Tomato;
  font-weight: bold;
  font-size: 30px;
  transition: 0.6s ease;
  user-select: none;
}
```

This places each arrow halfway down the picture.

This sets how long each picture takes to change.

We matched the colour of our arrows to the fox, but you can use any colour you want.

3. The 'previous' arrow will automatically appear on the left. Type the following to make the 'next' arrow appear on the right.

```
.next {
  right: 0;
}
```

4. Now you need to style your dots, including giving them their round shape. Type this.

```
.dot {
  height: 15px;
  width: 15px;
  margin: 0 2px;
  background-color: DarkGray;
  display: inline-block;
  transition: 0.6s ease;
  border-radius: 50%;
}
```

This makes the dots appear in a line.

border-radius adds rounded corners and **%** makes the dots totally round.

You can add the slideshow page to your menu bar using the 'pictures' button in your picture pack. (See pages 44-47 to remind yourself how.)

5. To make an active dot change colour, type this last rule. Save your style sheet.

```css
.active, .dot:hover {
  background-color: Tomato;
}
```

6. Now, go back to your 'pictures.html' file and run the page in your browser. You should now see an arrow on either side of the picture and three dots underneath. Try clicking on them to test your code.

If you want to add more pictures, you only need to add more HTML. The CSS and JavaScript stay the same.

CHANGE WITHOUT CHANGING

JavaScript makes your page interactive – so users can change things like which picture is displaying – WITHOUT changing the page itself. It does this using a kind of copy of your page known as a **document object model** or **DOM**. Each time the page is loaded, JavaScript can update and change the DOM copy without affecting your code. This is known as **DOM programming**.

GLITTERING STARS

Using just one image and JavaScript you can make any page on your website glitter with stars.

You're going to use JavaScript to take one image of a star and make it repeat all over your page very quickly. CSS will make the stars seem to glitter.

CREATE YOUR STARS

1. Choose a file and open it (we're using the homepage). First, you need to tell the browser where it can put stars. This means adding **<div>** tags that go around everything on your page.

```
<body>
   <div id="sky">

   </div>
</body>
```

> **id** is a kind of **class**. We've called it 'sky'.

MORE VARIABLES

JavaScript is used for lots of kinds of programming, so it has more than one kind of **variable**.

const (short for 'constant')
This has a fixed or CONSTANT value.

let This LETS the value change.

Both these variables only apply to the block of code where they are used, not the whole program.

2. Now for the JavaScript program. Add **<script>** tags between the closing 'sky' **<div>** and **<body>** tags.

```
   </div>
   <script>

   </script>
</body>
```

3. To tell the browser where to place the stars, you need to create a couple of variables, known as **const** variables (see box).

```
   const sky = document.getElementById("sky");
```

> The **const** is anything in the file with the **id** 'sky' – meaning the **<div>** tag you've just created.

Now you're going to write a function that uses the second **const** to decide where to place stars on the page.

> This bracket introduces the function you'll write next.

```
const randomNumber = function randomNumber() {
```

4. Add a **WHILE** loop to set when the function will run, and a **let** variable for it to use.

```
let r = 50;
while (40 < r && r < 60) {
  r = Math.random() * 100
}
```

> The loop uses the variable **r** and will run WHILE **r** is more than 40 and less than 60 (**&&** means 'and' in JavaScript).

> 'Math.random' gives a random number between 0 and 1. This is then multiplied by 100, so you end up with a number between 1 and 100.

5. Finish the function by returning **r** to its original value.

```
  return r;
}
```

6. Next add a FOR loop that will keep repeating as long as the browser's open. Type this.

```
for (let i = 0; i < 50; i++) {
```

> This loop uses its own **let** variable **i** to work out when it should run.

7. Create two more **const** variables for the last block of code. 'Delay' will control the timing of the animation. 'El' creates an HTML **<img>** tag to use in the JavaScript.

> This **const** variable will be used to work out how long the star appears in each position (**s** stands for seconds).

```
const delay = Math.random() + "s";
const el = document.createElement("img");
```

> This will be the star itself.

8. The browser also needs to know where to find your new **<img>** tag and the image itself needs a name so you can style it later.

This tells the browser where to find the image.

```
el.src = "images/star.svg";
el.className = "glitter-star";
```

This gives the image a name, or **class**, you can use in CSS.

9. The next two lines tell the browser how to position each star on the page.

'el' is the star from step 7.

'style' tells JavaScript to use CSS properties. 'top' and 'left' are CSS properties for positioning.

```
el.style.top = randomNumber() + "%";
el.style.left = randomNumber() + "%";
```

Each line uses the 'randomNumber' function to position the stars a random percentage (%) away from the top and left of the screen.

10. Now, tell the browser how long to show the star in each position. The code for this is slightly different for different browsers, so you need several versions.

```
el.style.animationDelay = delay;
el.style.msAnimationDelay = delay;
el.style.webkitAnimationDelay = delay;
el.style.mozAnimationDelay = delay;
```

These use the const 'delay' from step 7 to work out when to start each 'animation'.

11. Finish with a line telling the browser to 'append' or place the star inside the 'sky' **<div>** tags. Then close your function and **<script>** tags.

This is your star image.

```
    sky.appendChild(el)
}

</script>
```

When you have one HTML element inside another, they are known as a 'parent' and 'child'. Here 'sky' is the parent and 'el' (the star image) is the child.

This is the area of your page where your stars can appear.

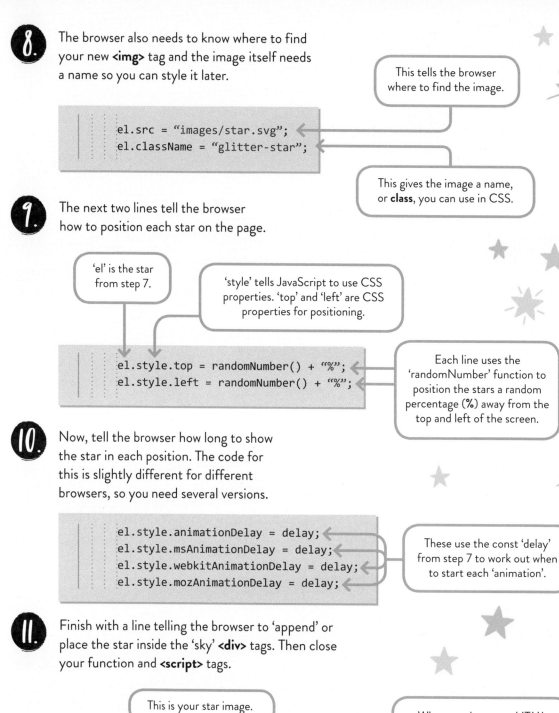

68

12. Your finished JavaScript should look like this. Check it and save your file.

```
<script>
  const sky = document.getElementById("sky");
  const randomNumber = function randomNumber() {
    let r = 50;
    while (40 < r && r <60) {
      r = Math.random() * 100
    }
    return r;
  }
  for (let i = 0; i < 50; i++) {
    const delay = Math.random() + "s";
    const el = document.createElement("img");
    el.src = "images/star.svg";
    el.className = "glitter-star";
    el.style.top = randomNumber() + "%";
    el.style.left = randomNumber() + "%";
    el.style.animationDelay = delay;
    el.style.msAnimationDelay = delay;
    el.style.webkitAnimationDelay = delay;
    el.style.mozAnimationDelay = delay;
    sky.appendChild(el)
  }

</script>
```

Now you have a page with stars. Turn over to find out how to make them glitter.

KEYWORDS

Words with a fixed meaning in JavaScript – such as
function, var, const, return – are known as **keywords**, or
reserved words, because you can't use them for names.
JavaScript is case-sensitive, so keywords need to be written
in lower-case or small letters. If you are using Notepad++
keywords will be *blue italics*. Numbers will be red. Inverted
commas (" "or ' ') and everything in between will be grey.

MAKE YOUR STARS GLITTER

To make the star 'glitter' you're going to make them change size and fade in and out. You do this with CSS.

1. Open your style sheet. Start by adding a rule to style the 'sky' – the space where your stars will appear.

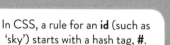

If only I were a REAL star...

In CSS, a rule for an **id** (such as 'sky') starts with a hash tag, **#**.

```
#sky {
  position: relative;
  width: 100vw;
  height: 100vh;
}
```

vw stands for 'viewport width' and **vh** for 'viewport height'. See the box below for more.

VIEWPORT

Your **viewport** means the browser window and how much of it you can see. **vw** and **vh** set the width and height of objects as a percentage of the whole window. If you make the window bigger or smaller, the object will expand or shrink to fit.

2. Then, add a rule to style the stars and animate them. You will need different versions for different browsers.

This means the stars can be positioned anywhere on the page.

```
img.glitter-star {
  position: absolute;
  height: 16px;
  width: 16px;
  animation: glitter 2s linear 0s infinite
  normal;
  -ms-animation: glitter 2s linear 0s infinite
  normal;
  -webkit-animation: glitter 2s linear 0s
  infinite normal;
  -moz-animation: glitter 2s linear 0s infinite
  normal;
}
```

glitter refers to an **at-rule**, which you'll write in the next step.

linear means the image will fade in and out evenly.

infinite means the animation won't stop until you close the browser window.

Using the **animation** property means you can style lots of things with one line.

70

3. Finally, add an **at-rule** to make the stars 'glitter' by changing their size and making them fade in and out.

```
@keyframes glitter {
  0% {
    -webkit-transform: scale(3.0);
    opacity: 1;
  }
  25% {
    -webkit-transform: scale(0.5);
    opacity: 0;
  }
  50% {
    -webkit-transform: scale(2.0);
    opacity: 1;
  }
  75% {
    -webkit-transform: scale(0.5);
    opacity: 0;
  }
  100% {
    -webkit-transform: scale(3.0);
    opacity: 1;
  }
}
```

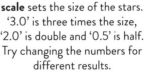

scale sets the size of the stars. '3.0' is three times the size, '2.0' is double and '0.5' is half. Try changing the numbers for different results.

opacity sets how see-through the stars are. 1 is fully opaque (not see-through at all) and 0 is transparent.

4. Save your style sheet. Go back to your HTML file and run it. It should now have glittering stars.

WRITE A QUIZ

As JavaScript is interactive, you can use it to make a simple quiz.

We're going to make a coding quiz for the Fox Hill Coders, but you can make your quiz about whatever you want. You'll need JavaScript to code the quiz itself and CSS to style it.

Our quiz will show the user three questions, each with three different answers. Users can click to select the answers they want, then click 'Submit' to see how they've done. The computer will then display their score, and the correct answers will turn green and the wrong ones red.

Let's play!

SET UP YOUR PAGE

Before you start coding the quiz itself, you need to create a page for it using HTML.

1. Open your new page template and save a copy as 'quiz.html'. Before the **<footer>** tags, open a **<div>** tag and add a few words to introduce your quiz.

> We've added the class 'quizzical' to the **<section>** tag, so it can be styled separately in the style sheet.

```
<div class="quizzical">
    <h3>Get QUIZZICAL with the Fox Hill Coders! Answer the following...</h3>
```

2. Now to lay out the quiz itself. You will need a section for the questions, a button to submit answers, and a section for the results to appear. Type the code highlighted below, and save your file.

> This is where the quiz questions will appear.

> This creates the submit button.

> This is where the results will appear.

```
<div id="quiz"></div>
    <button id="submit">Submit</button>
<div id="results"></div>
</div>
<footer>Made by A.Fox</footer>
</body>

</html>
```

BUILD YOUR QUIZ

1. As you will be handling a whole set of values (your questions and answers), you will need to arrange them in a form known as an **array** (see right). Open a **<script>** tag before your closing **<body>** tag and type this.

ARRAYS

In JavaScript, a variable is a way of keeping track of values. If you have a set of related values – such as questions and answers – you can keep track of them together by setting up an **array**.

> Square brackets go around the whole array.

> Each value is separated by a comma.

> This is the group of possible answers.

> The correct answer will link to an IF condition later in the code. IF an answer is correct, the text will turn green. ELSE the text will turn red.

> Curly brackets go around each group of values.

```
<script>
  var questions = [{
        question: "Who created the Fox Hill website?",
        answers: {
          a: "A. Cat",
          b: "A. Fox",
          c: "A. Spider",
        },
        correctAnswer: "b"
  },
  {
        question: "Which of these go around a CSS rule?",
        answers: {
          a: "{}",
          b: "[]",
          c: "()",
        },
        correctAnswer: "a"
  },
  {
        question: "Which one of these ISN'T a type of variable?",
        answers: {
          a: "const",
          b: "let",
          c: "return",
        },
        correctAnswer: "c"
  }
  ];
```

> We've written three questions, each with three answers. But you can add as many as you like, following this format.

```
{
  question: "WRITE YOUR QUESTION HERE",
  answers: {
    a: "ANSWER",
    b: "ANSWER",
    c: "ANSWER",
  },
  correctAnswer: "LETTER"
},
```

2. Now create three variables linked to the quiz, the results and the 'Submit' button, you created earlier. Type this.

This links to everything between the 'quiz' **<div>** tags – meaning the whole quiz.

```
var quizContainer = document.getElementById("quiz");
var submitButton = document.getElementById("submit");
var resultsContainer = document.getElementById("results");
```

This links to the **<div>** tags for the results.

This links to the 'Submit' button.

3. Now you need to call the function that will create the quiz, and then define that function.

This calls the function.

```
makeQuiz(questions, quizContainer, resultsContainer, submitButton);

function makeQuiz(questions, quizContainer, resultsContainer, submitButton){
```

This starts the function definition.

4. Inside the 'makeQuiz' function, you need another function to show the questions. You will also need variables for the way the quiz appears on screen (the output), and the answers.

```
function showQuestions(questions, quizContainer){
var output = [];
var answers;
```

5. Now you need to tell the browser what to do with each question and answer. This means using a couple of FOR loops, like this.

This loop tells the browser which question to look at.

```
for (i = 0; i < questions.length; i++){
answers = [];
for (letter in questions[i].answers){
```

This loop tells the browser which is the correct answer.

6. Add the code for the answer buttons and close the first FOR loop.

> .**push** here adds each answer to the variable 'answers' to create the results.

```
answers.push(
  "<label>" +
  "<input type='radio' name='question" + i + "'value='" +
  letter + "'>" +
  letter + ":" +
  questions[i].answers[letter] +
  "</label>"
);
}
```

> Each button goes inside an HTML **<label>** tag.

> The **radio button** is each answer the user can select. In HTML, a **radio button** is used when there are several choices, rather than just one button to select.

7. To answer a question, the browser needs to add that question and its answer to the 'output' (the 'output' will be what you see on the page).

> .**push** here adds each question and answer to the output.

> These lines create a space on the page for the questions and the answers (which you made in JavaScript).

```
output.push(
  "<div class='question'>" + questions[i].question + "</div>" +
  "<div class='answers'>" + answers.join("") + "</div>"
);
}
```

> This part 'joins' each answer to the rest in the array.

8. End the 'makeQuiz' function by telling the browser to add the results for each question together. Then close your brackets.

```
    quizContainer.innerHTML = output.join("");
}
```

> Don't forget – every opening bracket needs a closing bracket.

9. You've told the browser to collect the answers and work out the results, but you also need to tell it how to show them. Start a new function.

> These are the same variables you used before.

```
function showResults(questions, quizContainer, resultsContainer){
```

10. Next, add three more variables – one to collect the actual answers from the variable 'quizContainer', another to collect the users' answers, and a third to keep track of how many the user got right.

> This selects EVERYTHING in **quizContainer** with the name **answers**.

```
var answerContainers = quizContainer.querySelectorAll(".answers");
var userAnswer = "";
var numCorrect = 0;
```

11. Now, add a FOR loop.

> This loop will make the next bit of code run as many times as there are questions.

```
for(i = 0; i < questions.length; i++){
```

12. Tell the browser how to find which answer the user selected.

```
userAnswer = (answerContainers[i].querySelector("input[name=question"
+ i + "]:checked")||{}).value;
```

> || means 'or' in JavaScript. The | key is usually on the left of the keyboard next to the shift key.

> This looks for anything in 'answerContainers' that has been selected by the user – meaning the answer they have chosen.

13. The brower needs to know what to do when an answer is correct and when it is wrong. This needs an IF... ELSE loop.

> This checks if the user's answer is the same as the correct answer stored in your array.

```
if(userAnswer===questions[i].correctAnswer){
    numCorrect++;
    answerContainers[i].style.color = "lightgreen";
} else {
    answerContainers[i].style.color = "red";
    }
}
```

> If the user's answer is correct, their score will go up and the answer text will change to light green.

> If the user gets it wrong, the answer text will change to red.

14. Finally tell the browser what to show.

This shows the user's score.

```
    resultsContainer.innerHTML = numCorrect + " out
    of " + questions.length;
  }
  showQuestions(questions, quizContainer);
  submitButton.onclick = function(){
    showResults(questions, quizContainer,resultsContainer);
  }
}
</script>
```

This will show all the questions at once.

Make sure you've closed all your open brackets and closed your **<script>** tags.

This shows the results when the user clicks the submit button.

? ? ? ? ?

15. Your finished script should look like this. Check it and save.

JavaScript is **case-sensitive**, which means you need to type letters EXACTLY as you see them.

```
<script>
  var questions = [{
    question: "Who created the Fox Hill website?",
    answers: {
      a: "A. Cat",
      b: "A. Fox",
      c: "A. Spider",
    },
    correctAnswer: "b"
  },
  {
    question: "Which of these go around a CSS rule?",
    answers: {
      a: "{}",
      b: "[]",
      c: "()",
    },
    correctAnswer: "a"
  },
```

Turn the page for the rest of the code.

```
  {
    question: "Which one of these ISN'T a type of variable?",
    answers: {
      a: "const",
      b: "let",
      c: "return",
    },
    correctAnswer: "c"
  }
];
var quizContainer = document.getElementById("quiz");
var submitButton = document.getElementById("submit");
var resultsContainer = document.getElementById("results");

makeQuiz(questions, quizContainer, resultsContainer, submitButton);

function makeQuiz(questions, quizContainer, resultsContainer, submitButton) {
  function showQuestions(questions, quizContainer){
    var output = [];
    var answers;
    for(i = 0; i < questions.length; i++){
      answers = [];
      for(letter in questions[i].answers){
        answers.push(
          "<label>" +
          "<input type='radio' name='question" + i + "'value='" + letter + "'>" +
          letter + ":" +
          questions[i].answers[letter] +
          "</label>"
        );
      }
      output.push(
        "<div class='question'>" + questions[i].question + "</div>" +
        "<div class='answers'>" + answers.join("") + "</div>"
      );
    }
    quizContainer.innerHTML = output.join("");
  }


  function showResults(questions, quizContainer, resultsContainer) {
    var answerContainers = quizContainer.querySelectorAll(".answers");
    var userAnswer = "";
    var numCorrect = 0;
    for(i = 0; i < questions.length; i++){
      userAnswer = (answerContainers[i].querySelector("input[name=question"+ i + "]
      :checked")||{}).value;
```

The rest of the code
is on the next page.

```
            if (userAnswer===questions[i].correctAnswer) {
              numCorrect++;
              answerContainers[i].style.color = "lightgreen";
            } else {
              answerContainers[i].style.color = "red";
            }
          }
          resultsContainer.innerHTML = numCorrect + " out of " + questions.length;
        }
        showQuestions(questions, quizContainer);
        submitButton.onclick = function() {
          showResults(questions, quizContainer, resultsContainer);
        }
      }
    </script>
```

16. Save and run your file. You should see something like this. Try answering the questions.

If you run into problems, always check your code carefully, line by line. Most bugs are caused by typing errors or missing punctuation, which can be tricky to spot.

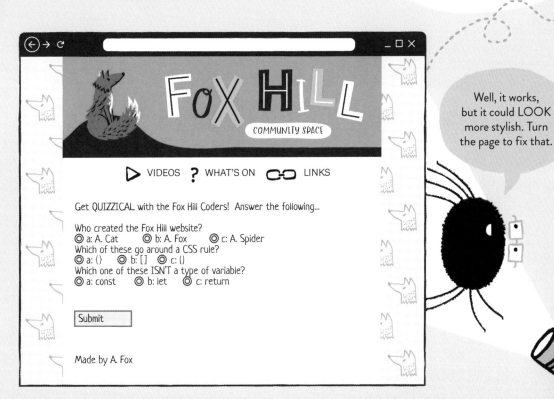

Well, it works, but it could LOOK more stylish. Turn the page to fix that.

STYLE YOUR QUIZ

You can style the layout of your quiz
and add a touch of colour using CSS.

1. Open your style sheet and add a few rules
for your quiz BEFORE the rules for your
glittering stars. First, add rules for your
questions and answers.

```
.question {
  font-weight: bold;
}
.answers {
  margin-bottom: 30px;
}
```

'font-weight' means how dark the
letters look. Setting it to **bold** will
make the questions look darker
than the answers.

This adds a margin below
each row of answers.

2. Now to style the 'Submit' button.
Type the following.

```
#submit {
  font-size: 20px;
  background-color: Gold;
  border: 0px;
  border-radius: 3px;
  padding: 20px;
  margin-bottom: 20px;
  font-family: Neucha, cursive;
}
#submit:hover {
  background-color: LightSeaGreen;
}
```

This gives the button a
colour, but no outline.

This gives the button
rounded corners.

This rule makes the button change
colour when a mouse hovers over it.

80

3. Finally, add a rule for the 'quizzical' **<section>** tag (the whole quiz).

```css
.quizzical {
  width: 50%;
  margin: auto;
  padding: 0 25px 40px 10px;
  border: 4px solid LightSeaGreen;
  border-radius: 5px;
  box-shadow: 5px 5px 5px DarkSlateGray;
}
```

This adds a coloured border. around the whole quiz.

This adds a shadow to the border you've added.

4. Save your style sheet and go back to 'quiz.html'. Run it in your browser. You should see something like this.

MAKE A SURVEY

A survey works very like a quiz, except that you want to keep a count of the answers. Here's how to use JavaScript to make a simple survey and store the results on your machine.

This survey will ask which activity should be added to the Fox Hill timetable – pottery or table tennis. Each option will have a button to click on. The survey will count how many times each button is clicked and store those numbers, even if the browser is closed. The survey will work on any computer that visits the website, but each computer can only store its OWN results – so this is best for a survey where users will be on the same device.

ASK YOUR QUESTION

(1.) Open your new page template and save a copy as 'survey.html'. Open a **<div>** tag under the code for the menu and add a header and clickable buttons.

> I vote pottery.

Using **<div>** tags keeps things neat and tidy. Adding the **class** 'innersection' means you can use the 'innersection' rule that's already in your stylesheet.

This line introduces the survey.

```
</ul>
<div class="innersection">
  <h3>Which activity do you want Fox Hill to add to the schedule?</h3>
  <p><button onclick="clickSurvey()" type="button">Click me if you want
  pottery!</button></p>
  <p><button onclick="clickSurvey2()" type="button">Click me if you want
  table tennis!</button></p>
</div>
```

These two lines add buttons to click on.

Each **onclick** attribute is linked to a JavaScript function you will write in the next step.

You can make your survey about whatever you want by changing the text in black.

CREATE YOUR ANSWER BUTTONS

1. Now for the JavaScript. Each button needs a separate function. This function will check if the browser allows storage (all browsers SHOULD, but it's good to make sure). It will then check if the button has already been clicked. IF both answers are yes, it will add one to to the votes. Begin by typing this between the **<head>** tags.

Click me if you want pottery!

Click me if you want table tennis!

> This loop checks IF the browser allows storage. **!==** means 'not equal to'.

```
<script>
 function clickSurvey() {
   if (window.localStorage!==undefined) {
     if (localStorage.potteryVotes) {
       localStorage.potteryVotes = Number(localStorage.potteryVotes) + 1;
```

> This loop tells the browser to check for previous clicks and add one to the votes. **localStorage** is the storage on your browser.

2. Finish the function by telling the computer what to do if the button hasn't been clicked or if the browser doesn't allow storage. If it's the first click on the button, the votes will be stored as 1.

> This bit of code only needs to run once. After the first time, it will be skipped.

> This line makes the number of votes counted display on your page.

```
     } else {
       localStorage.potteryVotes = 1;
     }
     document.getElementById("result").innerHTML = "Number of votes for
     pottery: " + localStorage.potteryVotes + ".";
   } else {
     document.getElementById("result").innerHTML = "Sorry, this survey doesn't
     work in this browser. Please try again with a better one!";
   }
 }
```

> This text will only appear if the browser DOESN'T allow storage.

3. Now for the second button. The code is exactly the same, except for the names and messages. Copy the whole function and paste it below the first. Then, change the highlighted text.

> You need to change the function name to link to the second button.

> You also need to change the text that displays when the button is clicked.

```
function clickSurvey2() {
  if (window.localStorage!==undefined){
    if (localStorage.tennisVotes) {
      localStorage.tennisVotes = Number(localStorage.tennisVotes) + 1;
    } else {
      localStorage.tennisVotes = 1;
    }
    document.getElementById("result2").innerHTML = "Number of votes for table
    tennis: " + localStorage.tennisVotes + ".";
  } else {
    document.getElementById("result2").innerHTML = "Sorry, this survey doesn't
    work in this browser. Please try again with a better one!";
  }
}
```

4. Add a closing **<script>** tag at the end and save your code.

```
</script>
```

SHOW THE RESULTS

1. You will also need a space for your results. Add two **<div>** tags and a line break like this, before your closing 'innersection' **<div>** and **<section>** tags.

```
      <p><button onclick="clickSurvey2()" type="button">Click me
      if you want table tennis</button></p>
      <div id="result"></div>
      <br>
      <div id="result2"></div>
    </div>
  </section>
  <footer>Made by A. Fox</footer>
</div>
</body>

</html>
```

> This displays the results for the first button.

> This displays the results for the second.

> I vote table tennis!

2. Finally, save and run your file. You should see something like this. Try clicking on the buttons and watch the counters change.

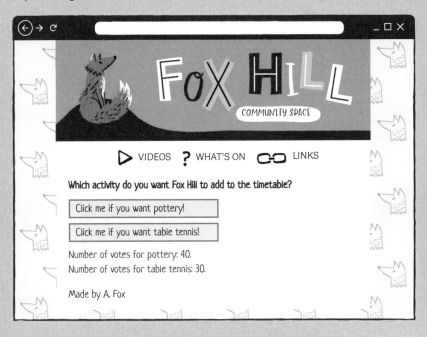

STARTING OVER

1. If you want to restart the survey, you will need to reset the votes. Add this line at the beginning of each function and save your file.

```
function clickSurvey() {
    localStorage.clear();
```

This clears the count.

2. Run the page in your browser again. The clicks should have reset to zero. Delete the line and save the file. Your browser will start storing the results again.

STORAGE AND SERVERS

This survey saves its results in the browser on your machine – so only people using the same browser on the same machine will be able to see them. To see the results from any browser on any machine, you would need to store the results online on a **server**. This requires a different kind of computer language.

Languages that control the mechanics you can't see, such as **server storage**, are known as **back-end** languages. They include **Python**, **PHP** and **SQL**. HTML, CSS and JavaScript, are known as **front-end** languages – meaning they affect what you SEE when you look at websites.

USEFUL STUFF

In this section you will find advice
about putting your website on the web,
as well as a glossary of the computer
words used in this book.

For links to websites where you can discover
all kind of resources for web design and
web languages, go to the Usborne Quicklinks
website at **usborne.com/Quicklinks** and enter
the keywords: 'build your own website'. You'll
also find downloadable files with finished,
working code for each stage of this book.

GOING LIVE

Before other people can see your website, you need to make it public by putting it on the **World Wide Web** – the network of linked pages which can be accessed by computers all over the world. This is known as 'going live'.

1. FIND A HOST

To put your site on the web, you will need to find somewhere to **host** it – meaning storing your files and allowing browsers to access them via an individual web address. Hosting is done by a dedicated computer known as a **web server**. You don't need a web server at home – there are lots of companies who can host your site for you. Some charge a fee, but many are free. Go to Usborne Quicklinks for more information and links.

Many sites require users to be a certain minimum age – so children may need an adult to do this for them.

www.foxhillcommunityspace.com

2. CHOOSE A WEB ADDRESS

Every website needs a web address, sometimes known as a **domain name**, so users can find it. The address often starts with **www** and could have various endings, such as **.com** (for a commercial site) or a country (for example **.co.uk** for the UK). You choose the bit in-between, but you can't use anything that already exists. Many hosting companies allow you to check which domain names are already taken.

3. CHECK YOUR FILES

When you're finalizing your files, it's a good idea to check you've got everything you need in one place and to run your HTML files through an HTML validator (see page 47).

Some code-writing programs have validators built into them.

CHECKLIST

☑ **HTML files**. Each page needs its own file. Your homepage file should be named 'index.html'.

☑ **Style sheet**. You need at least one CSS file to style your site.

☑ **Images**. Have you included the image files for all your pages?

☑ **Names**. Are your files named correctly? Do their names match the links in your HTML?

4. UPLOAD YOUR SITE

Now you should be ready to **upload** the files for your site. This means copying them from your computer onto your chosen web server. Exactly how you do this depends on the host you have chosen. Follow their instructions carefully to upload your site.

5. CHECK YOUR SITE

Once you've uploaded your site, you should check it works with different browsers and from different computers, including desktops, laptops, phones and tablets. Your site can now be seen by anyone with an internet connection, so you can ask friends and family to help you check.

TEMPLATES

The quickest way to create a stylish website is by using a **template**. This means a website that has been designed and coded for you – you just add the content. It's fast and easy, but you won't learn anything about web languages.

CHOOSING A TEMPLATE

Many websites offer a choice of templates. There are often hundreds to choose from, each with a different style or theme. Most templates are free, but you may need to pay for extras such as additional files or design changes. Some 'free' templates are really paid for by advertising, so you may have to accept adverts will be added to your site if you use them.

When choosing a template, think about how much you want to be able to change it. Some templates allow you to edit the code as much as you like. Others are unchangeable once you've put in your content.

USING A WEBSITE BUILDER

The easiest kind of template to use is known as a **website builder**. This takes you through creating a website step by step – and will host your site afterwards. The simplest builders you use by dragging and dropping text and pictures without seeing any code at all. This is good for people who aren't interested in learning web languages and just want a website. More advanced website builders may not give you as much help, but do usually let you see and edit the code.
ALL kinds of website builder will host your site.

DOWNLOADABLE TEMPLATES

Downloadable templates are the most flexible. These allow you to adapt the code yourself using a code-writing program such as Notepad++. A downloadable template usually comes as a type of file known as an **archive** (see right).

ARCHIVES

An **archive** is a way of compressing several files together, so you can download a group of files all at once. Before you can use the files, you will need to **unpack** them using an archive program. If you don't have an archive program on your computer, go to Quicklinks for help.

WIDGETS

Widgets are ready-made objects you can embed in your website without having to code them yourself (see pages 36-39 for more about embedding). There are widgets for everything from counters for keeping track of visitors to buttons that link directly to social media sites. Some widgets may also contain code you don't want – so only add widgets from sources you trust.

Go to Usborne Quicklinks for more information and links to downloadable templates, website builders and widgets.

GLOSSARY

anchor text The text on a **website** which **search engines** look at to check if any words match what they're looking for.

animation A series of images shown one after another, to make it look as though things are moving.

app Short for 'application', a computer **program** designed for a tablet or smartphone.

array In **JavaScript**, a kind of **variable** used to keep track of a whole group of related **values**.

at-rule In **CSS**, a **rule** that applies to the **CSS** itself, rather than the **HTML**.

attribute In **HTML**, gives you more information about a **tag**, for example, where to find an image that's being used.

back-end In **coding**, this means the things users can't see, for example, a server. Back-end languages include **Python**, PHP and SQL.

banner A large image across the top of a **web page**.

block In **JavaScript**, a section of **code** with the same **indent**, that runs as one unit.

brackets These group information together. **CSS** and **JavaScript** use curly brackets { }. JavaScript also uses ( ) and [ ].

browser A **program** which manages a computer's **Internet connection** and displays the information that goes through it.

bug A **coding** error which stops a **program** or **website** running properly or looking the way you intended.

button On a **website**, a small picture or shape you can click on to do something.

calling a function In **JavaScript**, asking the **browser** to run a particular **function** by typing its name.

camel case In **coding**, writing names without spaces, adding capital letters in the middle. Often used in **JavaScript**.

case-sensitive When capital (upper-case) and small (lower-case) letters are treated differently, so must be typed correctly.

class In **HTML**, an **attribute** added to a **tag**, so you can style it in **CSS**.

code Instructions for a computer written in a **computer language**, such as **HTML**, **CSS** or **JavaScript**.

code-writing program A **program** used for writing **code**, such as Notepad++.

coding Writing instructions for a computer.

computer language A language designed for computers, with a set word list and **syntax**.

CSS Short for 'Cascading Style Sheets'. A **computer language** used to **style** or set the appearance of **web pages**.

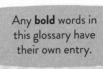

Any **bold** words in this glossary have their own entry.

data Information used by a computer.

debugging Fixing **code** to remove errors or **bugs**.

declaration block The part between {} in a **CSS** rule, containing a **property** and its **value**, for example 'color: red'.

DOM Short for 'Document Object Model'. A kind of copy of a **web page** that **JavaScript** interacts with to make the page **interactive** without changing the **HTML file**.

domain name A name used in a web address to identify a **website**, for example 'foxhill' in 'www.foxhill.com'.

DOM programming When **JavaScript** is used to update and change the **DOM**.

download To save something from the **Internet** onto a computer.

element The **CSS** name for an **HTML tag**.

embed In web **coding**, to include videos or other big **files** on your site by providing a **link**.

file A set of information saved on a computer. Different types have different letters or **file extensions** at the end.

file extension The set of letters after the dot in a **file name**, which tells the computer what kind of information is in the **file**. For example, '.html' is an **HTML file**.

file name What you call a **file** when you save it on a computer.

folder A way of grouping different computer **files** when you save them.

font A style of lettering – meaning the way the letters are written.

font family A set of **fonts** that look similar.

font stack In **CSS**, a list of **fonts** in a **font-family rule**. If a **browser** can't find the first font in the stack, it will use the next.

for In **JavaScript**, a **keyword** for a **loop** that makes the **browser** repeat a set of instructions a certain number of times. See also **loop**.

front-end In **coding**, this means the things users see, for example how a **website** looks. Front-end languages include **HTML**, **CSS** and **JavaScript**.

function In **JavaScript**, a complete section of **code** with one particular job.

hosting Storing **websites** and allowing **browsers** to access them on the **Internet**.

HTML Short for 'Hypertext Markup Language', the basic **computer language** used to build **websites**.

HTTP Short for 'Hypertext Transfer Protocol', a way of formatting information in order to send it across the **Internet**.

id In **HTML**, an **attribute** added to a **tag**, and used to refer to that tag in **JavaScript**.

if In **JavaScript**, a **keyword** used to test whether a **statement** is true. If it is true, the computer follows the next instructions. If not, it skips them. See also **loop**.

indent Adding a certain amount of space before a line or block of **code**. See also **nesting**.

input Information which you put into a computer or **program**.

interactive A **website** is interactive when a user can interact with it, for example by selecting or clicking on something. This uses **JavaScript**.

Internet A network of billions of linked computers across the world.

internet connection The link between a computer and the **Internet** – whether a telephone line, broadband or wireless (wifi).

IP address Short for 'internet protocol'. Each computer on the **Internet** needs an IP address, so other computers can find it.

JavaScript A **computer language** which allows you to add **programs** or **scripts** to a **web page**.

keyboard shortcut A quick way to do something using two or more keyboard keys.

keyword In **JavaScript**, an instruction word with a fixed exact meaning for the computer, such as 'Var'. Also known as 'reserved words'.

link An image or piece of text that takes you to another **web page** or **website**. A link that doesn't work is said to be 'broken'.

list A way of organizing information for a computer. **HTML** uses list **tags** to do this. See also **table**.

live When a **website** is **uploaded** to a **server** and can be accessed on the **Internet**, it is **live**.

local storage A small amount of **storage** available in your **browser**.

loop In **JavaScript** and other **programming languages**, a section of **code** that repeats. See also **for**, **if** and **while**.

markup language A **computer language** that tells a computer how to display or 'mark up' text and pictures. **HTML** is a markup language for displaying things on the **World Wide Web**.

menu bar A bar with **links** to all the main pages of a **website**.

nesting When you open and close one **HTML tag** or **JavaScript statement** inside another. Nested tags and statements should always be **indented**.

numeric code A way of encoding text by giving each letter, number or symbol its own number, which any computer anywhere can recognize.

output The results you get from a computer or **website**.

pixels The dots that make up a picture on a screen.

Python A popular **back-end computer language**.

program A finished set of instructions in a **computer language**, which tells a computer what to do.

programming language A **computer language** for writing sets of instructions or **programs**. **JavaScript** is a programming language.

property In **CSS**, something you can **style**, such as colour or size.

responsive When a **web page** changes size to fit the screen or device viewing it.

rule In **CSS**, a complete section for **styling** an **HTML tag**.

run To set a **web page**, **program** or section of **code** going.

save To store computer **files** so you can use them again later.

script In **JavaScript** and **HTML**, a mini JavaScript **program** you can include with your HTML by using <script> **tags**.

search engine A **website** that searches for information on the **World Wide Web**.

selector   In **CSS**, this selects the **element** you want to **style**.

sharing   Putting content, such as images or music, on your site for other people to use.

statement   In **JavaScript**, a single instruction, often starting with a **keyword**.

storage   The place where a computer or **program** stores **files**.

style   In **CSS**, when you set the appearance of a **web page**.

style sheet   All the **CSS** instructions for a particular **web page**. A style sheet can be a separate **file** (known as an external style sheet), or inside the **HTML** file (an internal style sheet).

style-sheet language   A **computer language**, such as **CSS**, that tells a computer how to present or **style** something written in a **markup language**.

syntax   In **coding**, a way of setting out **code** so a computer can understand it.

table   A way of organizing information in rows and columns, making it easy to compare and look things up.

tag   An **HTML** instruction inside < > . They usually come in pairs, with an opening and closing part. A few open and close in one.

template   An **HTML file** containing the **code** for a **web page**, so you can add your own content. Often provided by **hosting** sites.

upload   To send **data** or **files** from your computer to the **Internet**, usually so the contents can be used or viewed online.

value   In **JavaScript**, a value can be lots of things, including a number, word or **function**, and is stored in a **variable**. In **CSS**, a value is given to a **property**, for example the property 'font-color' can have the value 'blue'.

variable   In **coding**, a way of storing **values** that might change, like a box with a label. For example, 'const', 'let' and 'var' are all **JavaScript** variables.

viewport   The part of a **web page** users can see in their **browser** window.

wallpaper   A decorative background for a **web page**.

web page   A document you can access on the **World Wide Web**.

web server   A computer used to store and display **website files** on the **World Wide Web**.

website   A set of related, linked **web pages** with a shared **domain name**.

website builder   A tool for building **websites** without knowing any **code**.

while   In **JavaScript**, a **keyword** used to create a **loop** which repeats a set of instructions while a **statement** is true. See also **loop**.

widget   A ready-made object, such as a counter or **button**, that can be **embedded** in a **web page**.

World Wide Web   An enormous library of shared documents on the **Internet**.

INDEX

Edited by Rosie Dickins
Managing designer: Stephen Moncrieff
Additional design by Freya Harrison
Code tested by Jordan Akopojaro, Matthew Bugler, Lan Cook and Tom Mumbray
Additional coding advice: Voula Papadopoulos